The
Quiet Fields

Also by 'BB'

SPORTSMAN'S BEDSIDE BOOK
WILD LONE
MANKA
LITTLE GREY MEN
THE COUNTRYMAN'S BEDSIDE BOOK
IDLE COUNTRYMAN
BRENDON CHASE
FISHERMAN'S BEDSIDE BOOK
THE WAYFARING TREE
DOWN THE BRIGHT STREAM
SHOOTING MAN'S BEDSIDE BOOK
MEETING HILL
CONFESSIONS OF A CARP FISHER
TIDE'S ENDING
LETTERS FROM COMPTON DEVERELL
DARK ESTUARY
THE FOREST OF BOLAND LIGHT RAILWAY
ALEXANDER
MR BUMSTEAD
WIZARD OF BOLAND
AUTUMN ROAD TO THE ISLES
THE BADGERS OF BEARSHANKS
THE WHITE ROAD WESTWARDS
THE SEPTEMBER ROAD TO CAITHNESS
LEPUS THE BROWN HARE
THE SUMMER ROAD TO WALES
PEGASUS BOOK OF THE COUNTRYSIDE
THE WHOPPER
A SUMMER ON THE NENE
AT THE BACK O' BEN DEE
THE TYGER TRAY
THE POOL OF THE BLACK WITCH
LORD OF THE FOREST
RECOLLECTIONS OF A 'LONGSHORE GUNNER
A CHILD ALONE
RAMBLINGS OF A SPORTSMAN-NATURALIST
THE NATURALIST'S BEDSIDE BOOK

The Quiet Fields

'BB'

Illustrated by
D. J. Watkins-Pitchford
A.R.C.A., F.R.S.A.

Michael Joseph
LONDON

First published in Great Britain by Michael Joseph Ltd
44 Bedford Square, London WC1
1981

© Text by 'BB' 1981
© Illustrations by D. J. Watkins-Pitchford 1981

ISBN 0 7181 2039 6

Printed by Hollen Street Press, Slough from composition by
Alacrity Phototypesetters, Banwell Castle, Weston-super-Mare
and bound by Hunter & Foulis, Edinburgh

The wonder of the world
The beauty and the power,
The shapes of things,
Their colours, lights, and shades,
These I saw.
Look ye also while life lasts.

*For Valezina, Viscountess Bolingbroke
from James*

AUTHOR'S NOTE

This book might be termed the weekly diary of an idle man, one who has nothing better to do than jot down descriptions of a full year's rambling in the woods and fields; descriptions of the most trivial things, such as a passing effect of light, the shapes of ripples in a pond, dark trees against the sky at evening, all commonplace things which perhaps a great number of people would not notice. Yet it is these little things which make the passing days of a field naturalist intensely enjoyable, the very stuff of life itself. Indeed, W. H. Hudson found an admirable title for one of his most charming books, *A Traveller in Little Things*.

This book of mine might be termed the sum total of many of these 'little things' I have noted during the passing hours, from dead winter to spring and summer, on to golden autumn and winter once again.

My great hope is that the reader will accompany me on my rambles throughout the year, sit with me in my secluded garden or voyage with me on the bright waters when I go to catch a trout for breakfast, or just to watch the wildfowl which haunt the wet places. May he or she sense some of the delights I found in this still beautiful and wondrous world and perhaps feel with me a certain thankfulness to be alive.

'BB'
1980

INTRODUCTION

On Sunday the sixteenth of December 1979 two surprising things happened. Our postman, who sports sidewhiskers and has the face of a bishop, arrived at my window which was open to the bright morning and thrust into my hand a bundle of Christmas cards and one letter from my publishers.

It is a long time since we had a Sunday post. That was the first surprise. The second was to prove more dramatic. In the envelope from my publisher was a cheque for the equivalent of my fifteen years' teaching at Rugby School. I looked at it and thought there must be some mistake. It was a year's royalties for the Japanese edition of my book *Lepus the Brown Hare*, a most English tale of a Wiltshire hare from the time it was a leveret, snugged down in the mowing grass, to its subsequent life and adventures on the high downlands of that delectable Southern county.

The sum would be peanuts to property developers and industrialists, but to a scribbler like myself it was a fortune. That is why I am tempted to title this book *The Scribbling Lark*, which is really the country name for one of my favourite birds, that canary-coloured bunting, haunter of hedgerows, the yellow-hammer, whose eggs are scrawled with mysterious hieroglyphics and which, as a boy, I greatly prized in my modest collection of birds' eggs.

The postman is a friend of mine, who shares with me the hobby of collecting Bonzai (those trees in miniature which give so much pleasure). He had not had his Christmas box. I remembered I had lately purchased a book on the subject, so I called after him as he hastened back to his scarlet van and gave it to him, a mean return for *my* wonderful Christmas box.

The story of the hare had not taken me more than six months to write, and its sales in this country had not been

9

noteworthy. What, I wondered, had a People on the far side of the world seen in such an English story set in the quiet downlands of England? Animal stories are some of the hardest to write. If they are to live they must have in them a subtle something, a sum of hundreds of keen observations of nature and the ability to convey to the reader a vivid sense of the open air and the secret life of woods and fields. I must adopt a more fitting title for this book; I would do better to call it *The Quiet Fields*.

You may wonder why I harp on titles. They are supremely important to an author and his public and can make the difference of thousands of copies when the book finally reaches the shops.

It is in the quiet fields and woods of mid-England that I have grown up. They have coloured all my days, from when I was a small boy of seven, riding my pony about the misty pastures, up to the present time.

So I begin this book on 1 January, 1980. I intend to bring it to a close at the end of December unless some dark assassin lies in wait for me beside the way. It shall be a diary which will deal with the outdoor world, a catalogue of impressions, observations, a trick of light perhaps, the pearly ripples on my big pond, of ice and snow, maybe summer heats and smells, of butterflies, beasts, and birds — a hotch potch of impressions. What then have I for my first entry — a day of winter sun and bitter cold, with the frozen floods on the Nere water meadows shining like dull steel in the long valleys?

January 1

Towards this day's end, I made a visit to a most beautiful private water where greylag geese were grazing on the banks, a pack of wigeon with them. As soon as I looked over the boundary fence the geese were up and flying, showing their white half-moon tails, and the wigeon followed showing their white shoulders. One goose had been either pinioned or wounded, for it could not follow its companions but hurtled to the water, calling loudly. I saw a rare hybrid here not long since — a cross between greylag and Canada but, like all hybrids, not a patch on the normal plumaged bird. Hybrids are never satisfactory. One has only to look at the bird fanciers' efforts with bullfinch and gold-finch or goldfinch and canary. The colours are muddled, they have lost the artistry of nature.

The willows on the far shore glowed carmine in the low light, a sure sign that spring is not all that distant. The water was calm, cloven by the bright wakes of swimming fowl, mallards, and some shovellers, birds which are richly marked but ungainly in design with their long heavy bills. Tufted ducks rode with them, little tubby black and white people who wear a perpetual satisfied grin on their faces.

Great varieties have visited this lake. In the hard winter of 1978/9 three snow geese lingered long into the spring, stout-necked snow-white birds whose virgin plumage gave just the right artistic touch to the jet-black flight feathers, the distinguishing mark for the bird-watcher.

At this time of year the afternoon draws swiftly to its close, one moment a pallid sun shining from a bank of cloud, then a mist creeps over the water and distances become blurred.

On the roof of a farmstead a crowd of starlings were

11

chattering and gossiping. There were cattle steaming in the yard, and no doubt the birds had been gorging themselves on cattle feed. Soon they would be up and away in a compact mass to seek out their dormitory, and to that chosen roost others over a wide area would be converging.

Starlings *en masse* are the least attractive of our British birds and appear almost reptilian, but when I see one on a winter morning, perched on the old curved tiles of my garage with the feeble sun shining on its starred plumage, it presents a different aspect. With sun glinting on flanks and breast revealing flashes of purple and green, and with its bill wide open as it sings (no British bird opens its bill as wide when singing) it is almost beautiful. An ill-bred bird, rough in its habits, dirty also, but, like the house-sparrow, it has a certain lovable Cockney charm. It seems to enjoy life immensely, it is a clown of the bird world. Its song too contains all manner of clicks and whistles and very often the exact replica, on a more muted scale, of the songs of other birds, the fluting of thrush and chirp of sparrows, the latter a favourite part of its repertoire.

When I was a boy, there was a cowman who every evening called his cows home to the milking byre by a certain long-drawn whistle. The local starlings soon picked this up and sometimes deceived me by their mimicry on the gable top. In the half light of a winter's dawn I have plucked them from their roost in a great reed bed; they are unable to see in the dark and seem to be hard of hearing.

At the top of my garden there is an ancient apple, one of those old-fashioned trees which produce the most delicious fruit for pies. They are not keepers, you must use them swiftly, but no other apple is so delicious, either stewed or in a pie. They are, I think, codlings.

I have an early photo of this house, circa 1905, which shows the tree as a mere stripling.

Some ten feet from the ground is a hole where starlings breed each year. At about April time they arrive to take possession. There is always great competition for this nesting hole and rival birds have the most fearsome fights, rolling about on the lawn with claws locked together, uttering strident cries of rage. At such times I can almost pick them up, they are so engrossed in their battles. Later, the foolish birds often strew the lawn with new-laid eggs, being 'taken short' before reaching the nest hole.

January 3

Walking along a country road today I spied an ash plant growing in the hedgerow which had grown outwards and upwards, forming a perfect right-angle for a walking stick. I only had a blunt knife with me, but I set to work to sever it from the main stem. After a lot of hard sawing and cutting I did so, and found that when shortened it was exactly right for my hand. (I have a passion for nice walking sticks, though it cannot be termed a hobby of mine.) Somehow the handle fits naturally into the palm and is most comfortable. I cut a beech stick some thirty years ago in a wood in the Chilterns, and for a long time it was my favourite until I accidentally broke it.

One thing I have been unable to obtain anywhere is a ferrule. I have tried numerous shops but they all say they are unobtainable, which is puzzling as people still buy walking sticks and all must have ferrules on them.

I know that collecting sticks is a great hobby with many people, especially with shepherds and keepers. I once knew a retired Colonel in the New Forest who had a passion for them, all cut by himself in the forest and all beautifully finished and polished. Another man I know carves heads of badgers, foxes, pheasants, and other creatures which form the handles, though these are seldom comfortable in the hand and are only nice to look at.

Whenever I am out walking along the hedgerows I keep an eye for nice 'sticks'. I once bought a gorse stick in a pawn shop in Perth for five shillings. It is a fearsome-looking staff with a knotty top which almost forms a club. It is interesting to look at but not particularly comfortable in the hand. I often thought of its history. It was probably cut by some old Highland stalker or wandering tinker and served him for many years.

The winter-bare hedgerow always has a fascination for me, as in every yard there is something of interest, even if it is only the dead stalks of last summer's weeds, bleached white by winter frosts and winds, yet still delicate in design. Where the hedges have been laid, probably some dozen or fifteen years since, the old horizontal boughs are clothed with ivy which form cosy caverns for rabbits and hibernating hedgehogs.

I know I have written before of old birds' nests but I have such fun in identifying the architects. In the dead white stalks of 'gix' and nettles is the tiny frail hay basket of whitethroat, of garden warbler, and blackcap; it is amazing how such flimsy structures can withstand the winds of winter. The rather untidy mossy nests of greenfinch and hedgesparrow are fairly easy to recognise, and the easiest of all are the large structures of blackbird and thrush. Many are tilted sideways with their mud cups full of old berries, for the mice use them as larders.

It is amazing how common are the nests of goldfinches in my part of the Midlands; many are built on the outer sprays of elder bushes, (a favourite building tree) or in the upper thin wands of hawthorns and lower boughs of horse-chestnut. Here the nests are placed in an overhanging fork and are difficult to see; in any case they are little bigger than golf balls. These also withstand any amount of bad weather. The curious thing is that I seldom see the old birds about in the summer or hear them singing.

The frail platforms of turtle dove and woodpigeon stand out against the drab winter skies, these again so cunningly constructed that no wind can dislodge them, and they simply rot away. It may take more than a couple of years for old nests to disintegrate.

The nest of the bullfinch is unmistakable to my eye, frail rootlet-lined baskets nearly always fairly low down in the hedge and well concealed. An examination reveals perhaps

14

some empty eggshells which shows a mouse or jay has robbed the nest and sucked the eggs. Others, on close scrutiny, reveal blue quill casings and droppings and one can surmise the brood got safely away. The nest of the long-tailed tit is unmistakable, a little moss bag up in the thorns, but these rarely last to spring.

It is in this month of January that the woods and hedgerows seem to be most naked, before the buds begin to swell.

Walking along a country road it is very difficult to visualize the tremendous wayside summer growth which reaches its maturity in June. Last year (1979) the wayside vegetation was unusually high and thick due to the backward spring. When the warm weather came with a rush the grasses, ladies' bedstraws, and wild angelica grew as high as my shoulder — you could stand in some of the wayside margins and be almost hidden. Some of the hog weeds were over seven or eight feet high, so were the teazles. Now, nothing of that rich jungle remains but a few tattered dry stalks broken by frosts and flattened by the snows.

The same can be noticed around the margins of my Big Pond. The stately green flags with leaves like sword blades made a valiant forest; and pond-side willows, around which grew thickets of water forget-me-not, were sufficient to hide a brood of mallard; but now nothing remains above water save a few rotten sedges. The sparkling ripples which went chasing are sometimes gripped and frozen by a sheet of ice for weeks, (in the winter of '62 Big Pond was frozen from January to mid-March and I could walk or skate upon that grey expanse).

So at this time of year even the thick woods seem almost naked. I cannot believe I had to fight my way through barriers of brier and tall grasses to search for favourite sallows. Yet, when the leaves are off the bushes and trees the tendrils of brambles, which were once kept in check by the woodland rabbits (they relished the tender shoots), are as tough as a wire snare.

I had an instance of this when hedgerow hunting for pheasants last December. I was crossing a very deep ditch, so

15

deep I had to slither down to the bottom of it from a high bank. My right foot caught in a loop of bramble which held me as firmly as a snared rabbit.

I could not check my downward descent and finished upside down, firmly held by the ankle. I had to fumble for my pocket knife and lean forwards to sever the tough strand. I found it had formed a complete loop, one end of it having rooted itself firmly in the side of the ditch. Whilst I was sawing away with my knife a cock pheasant burst out of the dead grass in the ditch not five feet away and I was powerless to do anything about it.

Now that the hedges are cut by machine they lose a great deal of their individuality. They become dense, more like a suburban garden hedge, and the sapling ash plants have no chance to grow; in time wayside hedges will be denuded of trees.

It is not often realized that nearly all our hedgerow trees are bird sown. Oak, elm, ash, holly, and sometimes yew, which grace many of our road and field hedges are all sown by birds. The acorns dropped by jays and rooks tumble down through the intricate maze of branches and many find lodgement in the soil. The protecting jungle of twigs and herbage shields the tender saplings as they struggle up to the light. Once there they are well grown and capable of steady progress unless laid by the axe.

In some parts of the country, holly trees are quite common. You will notice that when one holly is growing you will find others in the vicinity, all sown by feasting birds. The woodpigeon is a great 'holly sower', so are the fieldfares and mistlethrushes.

A tree, or rather bush, which one sometimes sees in the hedgerow is the spindle tree, an unobtrusive thing until November when its delicate variegated berries shine out against the madders and purples of the bare winter twigs. The spindle is far from common about my home. In the spring I intend to strike some cuttings so I can have it in my garden, for anything that will give colour in winter is a joy. It is sometimes planted in pheasant covers, for the birds are fond of the berries, and where the position is right they will grow to a considerable height.

Where oak trees grow the jays and rooks are sure to visit them in the late autumn. It amazes me how jays and rooks can swallow the hard-shelled acorns. I do not think the jays shell them first — from what I have seen the acorns are swallowed whole. Woodpigeons will eat them too, but they are not so fond of them as are the jays and rooks.

These hedgerow oaks will sometimes retain their lower leaves until they are pushed off by the opening buds of spring, just as the beech will keep its lower leaves all winter.

Not far from my home the roads leading to a big estate are composed wholly of box, and in the Victorian era these were clipped close every year to form a neat continuous hedge. No barriers are so pleasant as box hedges and birds love to build in them.

January 7

Now is the time when hounds can expect a long hunt, for this is the clicketting season and the dog foxes travel outside their territory in search of their ladies. Most of the record runs have occurred after Christmas. The gasping coughing bark of the suitors is a familiar sound to me. On fine cold nights I often hear them in the forest close to my house. I remember walking home one night from pigeon shooting (in the good old days when pigeons flocked to the woods to roost), being accompanied on my way by a barking dog fox which seemed to be trailing me. It was quite an eerie experience. W. H. Hudson cites an instance when he was walking at dusk in the New Forest with two barking foxes trailing him for a considerable distance, one on either side of him.

The fox is one of our most timid and highly strung wild creatures of the countryside, and unlike the badger they can never get over their distrust of man. They do not make good pets and are even nervous of people who have reared them from cubs. They are graceful and beautiful animals when in their prime and certainly possess great cunning and intelligence.

I remember a Pytchley fox which had his kennel in the thick false growth of an old lime tree, and season after season gave hounds the slip by hiding up in this old tree. It was I who discovered his hideout when climbing one April day in search of jackdaws' eggs. The fox popped out of the mass of twigs just above my head, dropped to the ground as lightly as a feather and was away across the park. I never let on about his secret and believe that particular old rascal lived out his full span of life.

Way back in the fifties when pesticides were first used, many foxes perished. I was called to one which had fallen into the cellar of a house. It was partly paralysed and unable to stand. I got in touch with the huntsman from the Woodland Pytchley and he took the animal away in a sack for forensic investigation.

It had apparently been eating the dead pigeons which were strewn about the woods and had absorbed some of the dealdrin — the same poison which killed off the sparrow hawks and owls. I do not think the badgers were affected, as it is not generally an eater of carrion, but in any case the badger is such a secretive animal that some may have died in their setts.

What an amazing thing it is that nowadays foxes are becoming common in some of the suburbs of our cities! In most cases they are mangy beasts as they live on the contents of rubbish dumps and dustbins. So the suburban fox is a very different animal from the sleek healthy fox of the woods which has a gloss on his guard hairs and is in every way a more healthy animal, just as I believe that the country-dweller is more healthy than the townsman.

The fox and rabbit do not suffer like other animals when the weather is hard. The fox especially benefits, as birds and the smaller mammals are weakened by cold and the difficulty of finding food, so they can get rich pickings and there is always a regular supply of rats and mice round the stackyards. It is round the stackyards also that kestrels find their main source of food. When snow is on the ground one often sees kestrels sitting on top of ricks — this must make a change from the tedious method of hovering which always seems to me to be a most chancy and complicated way of earning a living. As for the rabbits, they grow fat on bark however hard the winter.

As I was writing this, the nice lad from the village (who had his own TV interview on New Year's Day) arrived on my doorstep with a young cock kestrel on his wrist. Way back in the summer he lost his other pet kestrel, but says it is always flying over his house and has even come down to make acquaintance with his successor.

He hopes to breed from his kestrels in his large outdoor aviary and has already bred tawny owls successfully. This little bird he showed me was in beautiful condition, with a gloss on its feathers, and seemed quite at home on the boy's wrist and not in the least nervous. Kestrels seem to have been virtually unaffected by the agricultural sprays, unlike the sparrow hawk which was wiped out in the midland area.

This leads me to the subject of hares. For some unknown reason hares are far less plentiful in Northamptonshire than formerly, and even on land where, in the past, one could be always sure of bagging one, they are now very thin on the ground.

One theory is that they have had some disease, but I have come across no dead hares in my wanderings nor have I heard of anyone else finding them about the fields. They are strange creatures, for though opposite my house there are large open fields which seem ideal 'hare country', they have never been common. Yet a few fields distant there used to be quite a number.

January 14 ───────────────────────────────

I had a phone call from the owner of the lake I visited on the first of January where I saw the 'hybrid' greylag snow-goose. Now this bird has been identified beyond all doubt to be the very rare dark version of the snow-goose which, as far as I am aware, has been rarely seen in this country. At first I could not believe this but on referring to the coloured drawing of 'Snows' in the AA Guide to British Birds there was the very bird, white neck and grey body, the grey darker on the back and with the same black flight feathers of the 'white' Snow. My host told me that it is not a recent visitor but has been seen on his lake for the last two years. I naturally thought it was an immature snow but now, beyond all doubt, it *is* the rare dark version. He asked me to come over and have another look at it. The day was not propitious. All lakes and reservoirs were frozen hard, and the sky was leaden grey promising snow. By the time I reached the Hall gates the flakes had began to fall.

Here my host awaited me with his head and underkeeper and we went down the side of the lake scanning the white expanse. Flocks of Canadas were standing on the ice and swimming about in an open lead but there was no sign of the dark Snow.

We then went on a tour of his three-thousand-acre estate. Leaving the valley we climbed away over wide fields where hares were chasing a doe, four of them all running one behind the other as they do in March. Pheasants stood about disconsolately and one or two partridge coveys, appearing like little round balls, crouched in the white expanse.

We came to another small lake, secret and remote, hedged with trees. I glimpsed the top of a boat-house, snow covered, and the lake itself, like a table spread with a white cloth. Most of the wildfowl had gone elsewhre, possibly to the Eye Brook or Rutland Water, but there was no sign of the rare snow-goose.

All around stretched the white bleak fields with here and there a solitary oak, one or two of immense size, quite likely the original trees in the Forest of Rockingham. The road we travelled was rough and full of bumps which would have jolted a landrover, but the Rolls in which we travelled so majestically transmitted scarcely a tremor; we seemed to float over the potholes noiselessly like a gliding boat.

By now the snow fell thickly, and we came down off the

hill in a blizzard. The head keeper has promised to let me know if the dark snow-goose makes its appearance and I will be over to take a closer look.

───────────────────────────────────────

Bob rang me up and asked me to go over to the river for a duck. At three-thirty I was at the farm and piled into the landrover with Fred Johnson, his dog, and Bob's little spaniel, a lovable little bitch who cuddled up close to me.

It was a bitter afternoon quickly drawing to dusk. White hoar frost masked each twig in the hedgerows, and the tall dead stalks of hog weed in the ditches with those fan-shaped tops appeared like fine white lace, every twig was furred with frost. Unlike the ride in the Rolls it was bumpy out to the water-meadows. We were thrown about like stones in a tin. We came to a stop beside a great tall hawthorn hedge with flat, fast dimming fields all around us. This hedge has not been laid for very many years so that each hawthorn bush had grown into a tall tree, favourite roosting place for the old cock pheasants.

Only a day or so ago all these flat fields had been two feet under water for they adjoin the Nene which curves away south-east from Oundle lock before turning to port and heading for the sea. Now most of the water had drained away, but it lay nearly a foot deep around the roots of the hawthorn trees. The cattle and sheep had worn hollows there in the far-off summer heats when they sought out shade from the burning sun.

It was strange to think of summer by that great ragged hedge. As we pushed through the knotted trunks to the far meadow the ice crackled and splintered like glass under our boots, a bad omen for the ducks' coming as it meant the remaining floods would also be skinned with ice. And so it proved.

Opposite to where I stood there was a large flash some

forty yards long by ten wide, the only sizable one in the field. I judged that if the duck came at all they would come to me. Bob and Fred went further down the hedge, and the dusk soon swallowed them up. On my left there was an immense thicket of thorns lining the bank of the river. To this, at intervals of a few seconds, went blackbirds, thrushes, and redwings, all passing over the frozen field for the warmth and shelter of that thorny barricade.

There comes a moment at flighting time when the mallard drake, resting on his daytime pond, river or lake, raises himself up and cries 'quar! quar! quar!' There is an urgency about that sound, as if the drake was asking a question, as perhaps he is.

Shortly after this repeated remark he leads his companions into the sky for their chosen feed for the night. I have noticed that ducks always seem to know where they are going, there is no wandering about the twilit sky, they are up and away, straight as a ruler, and usually it is the duck that leads.

I sensed that moment had arrived.

Looking across that dreary desolate field with its bare ragged thorn hedges, the frozen flood flash and the completely colourless evening sky, I knew that any second the ducks, if they *were* coming, would arrive. Sure enough, five wigeon appeared out of the gloom, circling and circling far out, each circuit bringing them lower and lower to the white blur of the ice. Finally they all settled in a rush, I could just see their dim forms on the margin of the flood, all alert and looking about them.

Whether they saw the pale form of my labrador by the hedge I do not know, but almost at once, they jumped and came past me at about fifty yards over the tall thorns.

I regretted then I had not brought with me the camouflage coat which I had made for the dog. It is amazing how a pale-coloured labrador (and Polar is a cream colour) stands out against a dark background. A few moments went by, then there passed overhead a great bow of wigeon. Ducks, unlike geese, do not often fly in a V, but nearly always in the form of a bow. As they passed over I heard them whistling softly to each other, a musical sound, nothing to do with the sound of the wind in their wings. They were far out of shot.

Then a bunch went over Fred far down the hedge. At the shot I heard the 'thuck' of a falling bird out in the field. In actual fact this was the only duck we had that night, for darkness came swiftly and with it the gentle rustle of falling snow.

January 20

It is one of those wretched mid-winter days which seems to have little to recommend it. The great forest some five hundred yards across the field by my house is shrouded in mist, and a wicked east wind sways the tall Irish yew outside my study window. I planted this, together with four others in my garden, by Little Pond some ten years ago. They were then some five feet high, bought from a nurseryman near Rugby to replace other Irish yews which I brought from my old home at Woodford Lodge. Those were twelve feet high but they died. The yew is a tricky tree to move and though I kept them watered during the summer they all turned a fiery rust colour and failed to survive. Now my present yews are taller and growing each year at the slow rate of six inches or so, for the yew, like the holly, is no fast mover.

I like Irish yews. Some people say they are funereal but this is not so. It is true they have a solemn dignity, but the birds love them both for nesting and for the very beautiful tapestry-red berries which they bear each season. The thrushes and blackbirds come for these berries and so, surprisingly, do the robins, who gulp them greedily and find it difficult to swallow them with their small throats.

Wrens and hedge-sparrows like to build among the dense upright branches, the wrens especially, though since the cruel winter of 1978/79 my resident wrens have gone. They suffer greatly in hard weather for their diminutive bodies cannot combat the great cold.

A yew hedge is the best of all hedges, better far than privet or thorn, but it takes fifteen to twenty years to make a good hedge. When I came first to my present home I needed a good barrier between my house and the road. I knew a yew hedge was out of the question as at my time of life one has to think about the relentless passage of the years. So from my old home at Woodford Lodge I transported, with great labour, some thirty well-grown privet bushes, each weighing the best part of a hundredweight, and I brought them here one at a time in my landrover. They each had a good mass of roots, for the privet makes a good root system, and I never lost one.

Now I have a dense hedge which I keep clipped, and it retains its foliage all through the year. Birds like it for nesting, and every year I have a nest of some sort, often a chaffinch, but usually a blackbird or two. In this same hedge I planted three trees, a laburnum, a silver-leafed sorbus, and a flowering crab. Upon these trees the resident sparrows sit about and gossip. I had little love for house-sparrows and at one time I discouraged them, for they are apt to harry my summer swallows which come every April's end to my garage. But I have now come to regard them as my guests, as I do all my other garden birds, and they now recognise this and do not stir when I pass close by.

At around four o'clock on these dreary winter afternoons they gather for a gossip and preen before retiring to bed, for they are early roosters. Long before dusk they have settled down for the night under the eaves of my outbuildings, creeping under the rafters and tiles. They have a certain winter chirp quite unlike that of summer. When the roads have been salted and sanded they settle on the surface in flocks, whether to eat the salt or the sand I do not know. I have noticed the same habit with rooks on the big motorways. Some time since, when travelling up the Great North road to Scotland, I have seen flocks of rooks on the margins of the motorway just when it is getting light, all feeding on the salted surface.

The small passerine birds go to bed very early in winter. Long before full dusk they are tucked up in bed. It is a long night for them, some fifteen hours, a good slice out of their brief lives. Thrushes and blackbirds go to bed much later, so do rooks and crows, which do not go to their roosting trees until it is almost dark, flighting time for the wildfowl.

Our wintering thrushes, redwings and fieldfares, will seek out those rough borders to lakes and reservoir where the summer grass has not been cut. It is warm down among the tussocks and, though they are in danger from hunting foxes, they are far more snug and warm than if they roosted up in the hedgerow trees. I have noticed, when wildfowling, how warm I have been, ensconced in the great reed beds bordering an estuary. The driving snow and bitter wind cannot reach you.

When I see my sparrows making ready for bed I sense a certain affinity with them: we each have our own lives and are ruled by the same needs, sleep and rest are necessary to our bodies, and without sleep we would surely die. Like me, they rise with the sun, and each and all of us go through our daylight hours with the same need for a warm retreat at night, and food for bodies' fuel. What a strange mystery is this whole business of living!

My resident tree-sparrows are rather secretive and aloof little people who consider themselves a cut above the house-sparrows. Their black spot on the cheek is like a caste mark, and their rich chestnut heads are quite distinctive from the grey heads of the house-sparrows. They do not go about in large flocks, nor, as far as I can see, do they indulge in those dreadful squalid brawls in the gutter in which the male house-sparrows indulge when after a particularly alluring hen.

House-sparrows are great ones for making an affray — everyone diving in like rugger players into a scrummage, chirping in vulgar fashion. In fact, it is the high pitched quarrelling chirp which often attracts the attention of other sparrows who may be in the vicinity, then everyone joins in. They are sometimes so engrossed in their wrangles that you can almost put your hat over them.

I know my little birds so well, the finches and sparrows, that I can tell by their eyes when they are happy or scared. A frightened bird opens its eyes very wide, but when friendly and content the lower eye-lid is raised a little, a real smile as I see it. Whether the hawk family or the owls can show this I very much doubt as the birds of prey have round staring eyes, deceptively lidless. It is the birds of prey which have the most beautiful eyes of all wild birds; they shine like rich gold with a dark iris. The heron and bittern also have this staring eye, as do many of the sea birds, the gannets and gulls.

January 22

In my kitchen garden I have a grove of small sallows which I have struck from cuttings taken last March. The sallow is not difficult to strike as it is of the salix family. I cut about a dozen large branches and staked them well, pushing them in quite deeply into the soil. By the end of May all had leaves and now, in their second year, they are well-grown trees.

They are my stock for my caterpillars of the rare purple emperor butterfly which I keep in a muslin cage. The process of bringing these larvae through from egg stage to the release of the butterfly in the wild I have dealt with in my book *Ramblings of a Sportsman Naturalist*, which was published in 1979 by Michael Joseph.

At this time, mid-winter, I have around eighteen tiny larvae hibernating on the stem of my growing sallow in the cage. Three elected to hibernate in the folds of dead leaves which I have had to wire to the parent tree. These minute creatures, which exactly resemble the grey green wrinkles in the sallow bark, are almost impossible to see unless you know the precise place where they are located.

The favourite site for hibernation is just where a branch joins the main stem. The bark is always a little wrinkled there and they like to hibernate low down on the main trunk. I suppose they do this in the wild, though I have never found them thus in the woods. Moreover, they like to meet together. In one angle of a branch I have no less than six, all sleeping like little boys in a dormitory.

The other day, on looking carefully at the muslin tied below the tree to prevent the entrance of earwigs and spiders (which are deadly enemies to caterpillars of all kinds), I saw to my dismay that two had somehow fallen off or, what is more likely, that they had been on some of the dead leaves which had dropped way back in October. Now here was a pretty pickle! If I left them there on the muslin they would surely perish. The problem was how to get them back on to the parent tree.

Luckily at that time we had a few very mild days, so the tiny creatures were not deeply asleep. I managed to get the edge of a leaf under their heads and, with a lot of coaxing and pushing, I persuaded first one then the other to crawl on to the leaf. This was a most delicate operation as so fragile a thing, far shorter than my little fingernail, could be so easily damaged.

Once on the leaves they began to crawl around and I bound the leaves by the stalks on to a main branch of the sallow. All was well. Within a few minutes both had left the leaf and sought out a more secure hibernation place on an angle of a branch.

How difficult it is to visualize what changes come to those minute creatures! First, when they awaken in the spring, they will grow swiftly to become as long as my thumb and half as fat, strange slug-like larvae, a soft green in colour, and horned like bulls. Then at the end of June comes the great transformation to the chrysalis and, finally, the grand emergence in mid-July, when the perfect insect takes wing into the forest.

I have written at such length about this grand rare insect in my former book that I will not do so here, suffice it to say I have managed to establish it in a Midland forest where it has not been seen for half a century.

The satisfaction this gives me is immense but it has meant hard work and great powers of observation, first in finding the eggs in the wild, and then securing egg and leaf to the growing tree. I was rewarded in the summer of '79 on one hot July afternoon by seeing three or four of my precious purple emperors disporting around the crowns of the forest oaks, a sight few naturalists have witnessed.

The immense green field, close cropped as a lawn by grazing sheep, was bathed in the morning sun. On the far side was a tall ragged hedge of thorn not laid for many years, with here and there a bird-sown tree along its length, mostly field elms, dead with the elm disease, bare dead poles like those on a wartime landscape. This huge green expanse made an immediate impact on me, there was a sense of great peace. No hint of coming spring in the air, even though it was so warm (I did not need an overcoat). Nor was there a sense of winter, but a noticeable rarity about the atmosphere. I will not use that cliché, the air was 'like wine', but there was a purity about the bright morning, a sense of delicious freshness.

Far out in the centre some gulls were sitting about enjoying the warming rays and from time to time they cried out 'keeze! keeze!' — a seaward sound. There were rooks also but they did not seem to be feeding, they were revelling in the brave morning. They were standing about on the grass.

Their enjoyment of life was matching mine. I have never seen grass so finely clipped in winter — it resembled a gigantic golfing green. At the far end of the field a flock of sheep were grazing, the only creatures intent on filling their bellies.

As I leant on the five-barred gate surveying this quiet scene I was aware of a curious fairy music and was puzzled as to what it could be. I find it difficult to describe the sound. I can only liken it to distant tinkling water music — it had a liquid quality and yet, intermingled with it, was a faint hissing, a strange murmur.

And then I saw that behind me, across a narrow pasture, there was a thicket of thorns with here and there a willow, red twigged in the sun. Among the branches of these thorns was a great company of redpolls, they were all singing in unison just as starlings do at twilight. They were singing out of the pure joy of living and praising, if you like, that peerless morning, when not a single cloud was in the sky.

No doubt if the rooks and gulls could sing they would

29

have done so too. They found their contentment and joy in resting on the close-cropped sward. When the sap is really moving in the sward, and the trees and hedges, you can smell it. It is the faintest of perfumes unless you put your nose right down in the warm grass and then it is quite strong. But on this morning there was no hint of it, only the faint smell of damp leaves in the wayside ditch which had been newly cleaned out.

Through my glasses I could see right across the field to the far hedge and saw what the naked eye did not reveal, something moving under the thorns. It was a cock pheasant. In a few days now he should be safe from the sportsman's gun; his only enemy will be the poacher out for something for the pot or a marauding fox. The fox will lie in ambush like a lion and spring on his prey, he will never course game like a dog.

It amused me to observe this cock pheasant which was quite unaware he was being watched. Through my powerful glasses I could bring him almost in range of a gun. Now and again he would stop and look at the birds out in the field, then resume his stately walk up the ditch pecking here and there. He came to an oak, a fine big tree whose branches spread low over the grass, but it was far too late for acorns — they had been gathered long since way back in the autumn days. But he searched carefully about, his round red-brown eye searching between the fallen leaves and grass blades and once he scratched at the leaves like a hen. Perhaps he had memories of past golden October afternoons when he filled his belly there.

A bunch of green plover came sailing over the tall hedge, their rounded wings winnowing the air, not purposefully like a pigeon or blackbird, a veering lightsome flight. One by one they alighted delicately in the centre of the field. There they ran about dipping their crested heads from time to time to snatch some minute something from the grass. Green plovers never seem to rest, but are forever running and stopping. They are beautiful creatures with their fine crests which blow in the wind like weathercocks, and their silvery breasts showed up well against the green background. Somehow there is something foreign about the plover tribe. In the old days sportsmen shot them for the pot and very good they are on the table, but better seen in that quiet green field! These huge pastures are visited by golden plover in the spring; large flocks will linger for a day or so before journeying north for the high moors where they breed.

With the sky completely clear of cloud the regular traffic high in the stratosphere was discovered. Thin silver pencils as transparent as those gauze-winged flies that haunt our summer streams were revealed on their regular journeys, each leaving in their wake a long double line of vapour which stretched from horizon to horizon. On days when cloud obscures the upper atmosphere we do not see these voyagers of the air which travel across our skies with the regularity of trains. They are so high that even the rumble of their passage is hardly heard. Yet watching that thin silver pencil gleaming in the rays of the morning sun I could not help wondering if man's conquest of the air has done him much good in the long run, and I *mean* the long run.

Does it profit us to get to our destination any more quickly? I hardly think so, unless it is a case of medical attention. Strange to think that up there was a crowd of my fellow men and women, sitting as comfortably as in a theatre, but seeing nothing of the world beneath them and hardly conscious of any forward movement. I watched the vapour trail float and curve and die and felt no envy for those travellers in time and space.

January 31 _____

My old friend, whom I called the 'Professor' because of his rustic wisdom, is no more. Only the other day I took him in to the local hospital for treatment. Now he is gone.

When I was making one of my ornamental ponds I enlisted his aid for his judgment of levels and the ways of water was profound. For many years he had been a gardener at the local squire's and he had a fund of tales which I was to hear again and again over the years.

One concerned the mucking-out of an ornamental pond close to the 'big house'. This had not been cleaned for many years and there was three or four feet of mud in the bottom of the enormous concrete basin. When at last the task was nearing completion, a writhing was observed in the glutinous stinking mud. With the help of grooms and gardeners there was extracted the grandfather of all eels which weighed something in the region of twelve pounds.

The professor pruned my roses every year, and the climbing rambles on the house were always a joy to see after he had done the job. From time to time he brought me gifts, spring cabbage plants, and once a bag of small onions because he understood I liked them. 'Something to gnaw at,' he said, thrusting the bag into my hands.

And then the other day he stepped out of his cottage door on the banks of the stream which bounded his plot (and where he caught gudgeon and minnows for me in the summer evenings) and fell forwards into the dead stalks of the Michaelmas daisies and died. His tearful widow showed me the flattened herbage where my old friend had fallen, such a poignant flattening of stalks. Yet that was the way he would have wished to go, with no long suffering imprisoned in a hospital bed.

His family is certainly the most ancient in the village. He could trace his ancestry back to the sixteenth century when all the land about here was a vast forest. There is a story in the parish records of a sixteenth-century parson being convicted for poaching a deer and I seem to remember an ancestor of my old friend was concerned in it. The name of Mayes is one of the earliest on the parish records.

My old friend helped me plant two Lombardy poplars when I first came to my present house. These were originally in an outdoor aviary at my old home and I took the tops out of them to keep them within bounds. They were then no taller than eight or nine feet. Now they are enormous, towering away into the sky, and must be quite eighty feet high — this being a growth period, since they were planted here, of some fifteen years. Lombardy poplars like to get their roots down into the water table and as there is a stream some twenty yards away they have evidently found the place to their liking.

In Gilbert White's *History of Selborne* he describes planting a Scotch fir and seeing it top the roof of his house. I did the same with my poplars, noting the time I saw the first leaf just begin to show over the tiled roof of my garage, and now they have reared their silvery green spires high above. They must surely be one of the fastest-growing trees, and in this they resemble the balsam poplar which has always been a favourite tree of mine. In early spring the sweet honeycomb smell of the opening leaves is at times almost overpowering, but it is a beautiful scent, redolent of summer.

Both my balsam poplars were originally two small branches broken off a tree in the centre of Salcey Forest years ago. I cut these branches in the spring and they rooted and grew several inches even in the first year. Now they are almost as tall as my Lombardies.

Even in the dead of winter you can catch the scent of summer if you roll the sticky buds between your fingers. All the poplars are the favourite food plant of many of our moths, chiefly hawk moths, and every year I can find the large green larvae on my trees.

If one has passed one's half century and wishes to plant a tree, it is somewhat depressing to know you will never see it reach maturity. One of the blessings of the present age is that one may now obtain well-grown trees, fully rooted, from good nurserymen, but even so you must choose with care if you wish to see them blossom. The nineteenth- and eighteenth-century landowners did not think on such selfish lines, they planted for their descendants and could no doubt visualize the finished landscape as it would appear a century later.

If one is close on seventy then one must also reflect on the wisdom of buying a dog. This I find even more depressing, for the dog may well outlive you.

These last few days of January have been delightfully sunny and mild yet Big Pond still remains frozen, with a film of water swilling on the surface. It is, I fancy, waiting for more frost and snow, and February is upon us, a month for which I have little regard. For the sportsman, unless he be that hardy breed the coarse fisherman, has to wait for the trout, though in some northern and southern streams there are grayling to be caught, a fish I have never caught nor seen in this country, but only in Austria where it was considered a better fish than the trout. I caught a very large one under the wiers at Gmundun in Upper Austria before the war, and my 'lederhosen' ghillie danced with joy when he inserted it into his little wooden barrel.

There are so few hints of spring in February apart from the lengthening twilights, no green appears on the hedges, and only the honeysuckle bines show green in the woods. Just as at summer's end in August the fields and woods seem weary and lifeless, so in February that sense of deadness still remains. For the shooting man also it is a dead season unless there are pigeons to be shot, and now, in my part of the world, wood-pigeons are few and far between. I miss my evening forays in the roosting woods — it is some time since I tasted pigeon pie!

February 2

Just as I was reading a piece of mine which appeared in the *Shooting Times*, bewailing the absence of my family of moorhens from my garden pool (where they had resided and bred for three or four years), daughter Angela announced 'the moorhen's back!'

Unbelieving, I went to the window and there he was (or she, it is hard to tell the sexes apart) perched on the stone staddle stool by the Big Pond, his favourite perch. For seven long months he has been absent. Where could he have been? Moorhens move about the country and will even go to the coast when the weather is hard. Anyway, here he was back again, large as life and quite at home. When I went to greet him he came to be fed with chickcrumbs.

As my resident moorhen family reared at least seven broods over the years on Big and Little Pond in my garden, this new arrival may well have been one of the younger ones, though it looks to me like one of the original old birds. I am delighted to have him back and hope that 'come spring' he or she may lure a mate into the garden and set up house, as of old, on Big Pond.

The yearly raising of babies was a constant source of pleasure to me, from the moment the old birds built their nest within yards of my french windows, to the time when the little black puff balls emerged to be tended by their parents with great solicitude. For moorhens, though they may be savage to other species trespassing on their territory, are devoted parents. If by chance they should elect to have a second brood then the young of the first turn to and help with the feeding. I know no other British bird which will do this.

What a pleasure it is to welcome back old friends after a long absence! The bird-watchers of Slimbridge must feel the same when the whooper swans return each year, one has been returning for fifteen years, making the long journey with all its perils from northern Russia. To my mind there is great romance about a great bird like a wild swan. What sights it must have seen in the lonely places 'where no man comes', what glorious dawns and sunsets it must have seen, what vast journeys over remote lakes and tundras. When the silver birches in the barren lands show saffron yellow and the first frail skins of ice cover the open water, then what magic it must be to rise with one's beloved (swans mate for life) and begin the journey to far Severnside where they know a friendly welcome awaits the devoted pair! Just as a shepherd knows his sheep, so the wardens at Slimbridge know their swans. The wild ducks, I suppose, are a different matter, unless the rings can be read on their legs, for all mallard (to us) look alike. But the wild whoopers and berwicks have recognizable bill patterns, not one is alike, just as our fingerprints are unique. No doubt also, to those who have grown familiar with them, the faces of the swans are different also.

I should like to know the exact route which the wild swans take from Russia. It must pass over perilous ground. Even in this country there are cad gunners who would think nothing of shooting a wild swan. Their strange unearthly calls add greatly to their mysterious charm. I remember hearing a flock pass over me one moonlight night when I was camping up Glengarry in late autumn. I was sitting by my camp fire and the night was very still. The loch lay like a sheet of silver under the full moon and the sound came from the east, at first faint, then swelling louder as the great white birds passed overhead. No doubt they had just come in and this was the end of their long journey.

A few years ago a wild swan was something to be excited about when one visited a Midland reservoir in winter. Now most large stretches of open water have wild swans every year and the numbers on the Ouse Washes grow every year.

I have said before how much I dislike this month of February, it really has little to recommend it. There is yet no real sign of spring save for the little white points of the snowdrops just peeping through the grass under my old apple trees. I have heard rumours of aconites in flower down in the village, but mine have not yet shown any sign. In any case, the sour yellow of the aconite does not suggest spring to me as does the primroses' tender yellow, or the golden club of the crocus, though I hope to see the latter within a matter of three weeks or so from now.

A mole came again yesterday. The trap was sprung, the run filled in with new earth. He must be a very sagacious mole indeed, for I am a dab hand at catching them with the well-tried ring traps.

Today the sky is a dirty putty colour. Occasionally spits of rain made rings in the wayside puddles up the country lane, not a bird whistled, a mean wind rocked the slender branches of ash saplings in the tall hedges.

I saw a brown object lying beside the road on the tangled wet grass. It was a hen pheasant which had been hit by a car, and that recently. It was not badly marked so it was quickly in my poacher's pocket. Some people would hold up their hands in horror at picking up a dead game bird for the table but I have no qualms about it. Only recently a car in front of me bumped a cock pheasant which foolishly ran across the road. The car did not slow and so I had another free meal.

What amused me was that some way along the lane a shabby van was drawn up in a gateway and scrawled in the dirt on the back-board was some graffiti which read: HISSING SID DIDN'T DO IT. This cryptic message had of course no connection with the bird in my pocket but I could not help speculating *what* it was that Hissing Sid did not do. One can sometimes see highly amusing graffiti written in the dust and dirt on the backs of lorries, the humour is particularly British. The gentleman apparently asleep in the driver's cab with cap over eyes was possibly Hissing Sid himself. We did not enquire but left him sleeping.

A mile on down the road, past the wood where years ago I shot pheasants with the old squire, our local Baronet, there was a grumbling and chuttering sound which echoed through the sad and misty trees. A helicopter was spraying a field, swooping and diving like a gull at a plough tail.

It alighted gently as an autumn leaf on the field over the hedge, the long swinging blades rotating ever more slowly until they drooped like wilting bluebell stalks. The perspex door of the round bubble cockpit opened and a young fellow emerged in gum boots carrying a thermos flask. I wondered what the old farmer, long dead, would have thought of this strange apparition sitting on his field!

I would have conversed with the pilot, but he was too far off even for a shouted conversation and it had begun to rain again out of the dismal grey sky. We went back through the wood.

Not a trace of green anywhere in the gleaming tangled thickets, the bare ash poles, and the spreading oaks. Each thorn and twig wore a silver drop of water and grey smears of puddles stood among the thickets, for this wood is a boggy one. Old blackthorn bushes, dense, dark and top heavy, formed mysterious caverns of purple-black shadow and against the sombre shades paler bare branches crossed and recrossed, an intricate web of thorns. These ancient thorn thickets are dog-proof even to terriers and it is into them that hunted pheasants creep and are safe on shooting days, even lying low under the belabouring of beaters' sticks.

One narrow ride, which was scored with sad ribbons of standing water, reminded me of a far-off winter's day when all was frost and snow. It was halfway down it that I shot three pheasants one after the other and saw an old dog fox. On that same winter's day we had the last drive close to the Hall. I stood in the road by the drive gate with the squire just behind me (his shooting days were over but he still came out with guns to see what manner of shots we were).

A very high pheasant came twirling over the oaks and at my shot it fell 'dead as a hammer' as old Colonel Hawker would say, not thirty yards from us at the side of the drive. When at last the beaters came out of the plantation this pheasant could not be found, although it was manifestly 'dead in the air'. The dogs feathered around in the shrubberies and up the drive without result so I walked across to where I thought it had fallen and, parting the bracken and grass, disclosed a fern-filled brick well some two feet square. At the bottom, dimly seen, was a pheasant's tail. The bird had gone straight down into this aperture head first.

A wounded pheasant will often take refuge in a rabbit hole, and so will an unwounded bird on occasion, but this was a dead bird. They have exceptionally keen hearing, as many a sportsman may have noticed, and will begin to move forward as soon as beaters begin to assemble. They have keen hearing and eyesight and can, I believe, see as well as a man.

In the narrow road with the wood on either hand we were sheltered from the grey wind, but looking up to the tops of the trees, I could see the thin ash poles swaying and creaking and the maze of topmost oak twigs shifting under the buffet of the mean wind.

In high summer this road is fringed with acres of meadow sweet, and in the glades spires of willow herb make a mist of rose. There is no looking into the wood's heart then, all is an impenetrable wall of leaves. I once thought I saw a purple emperor here which must have strayed from the great woods to the east. It was afar off so I could not see its colour but it soared and glided with the unmistakable flight of this rare and lovely insect. No other butterfly flies like it, for after a few quick beats of its pied wings it glides around like a fulmar on the coastal cliffs.

It is down this road that I hope to come in four weeks' time, choosing a day when the sun is warm and air is still, for it is here I see the first brimstone butterfly. I look for it as eagerly as I do for the first swallow.

Over the years this lane has never failed me. What a joy it

is to see the flicker of yellow wings as the butterfly comes plodding along the woodside where the sallows are showing white and golden buds. A day in early spring, when the first bees are out, then is the hour to look for the brimstone. It is a butterfly which, for some reason, seems as plentiful as ever, unlike the red admiral and the wayside butterflies of yesteryear, the small coppers, marbled whites, and meadow browns. It is difficult to say why we have lost so many of our butterflies, heaven knows we have a small enough list compared to most other countries. The silver-washed fritillary is now unknown in the great woods where I used to see it in abundance, yet the wild violet on which the larva feeds is still there on the sun-warmed banks and glades.

The wayside butterflies were probably killed off by marginal spraying, but there has been little spraying in the woods. Yet what of the deadly mist from that hovering helicopter and spraying plane, which is now such a common sight each year in my part of the country where farming is intense? Cannot that same shrill wind of this morning carry the spray into the woods? The air must be full of it.

One thing I sadly miss at my present home is the absence of green grass pastures. Every year it is corn, barley, potatoes, beans, peas, never the soft green grass like my Quiet Field where I so often go.

You see no birds among spring corn save maybe a solitary lark or questing pheasant. I miss the sight of the green plover flocks, the nodding woodpigeons, starlings, rooks, fieldfares, and redwings which used to flock every year to the forest meadow by my house, and where, each April, my old friend Tub (now turned keeper) used to tend his sheep and lambs.

My moorhen has left us again. When we looked out this morning there was no little black figure hurrying down the lane for his breakfast. I hope no fox has had him in the night or that a motor car is responsible. What makes matters worse is that I had ordered another consignment of chick meal which arrived before we got up this morning. Perhaps the sudden vision of the man carrying the sack scared him off, but if we get some hard weather again he may be back. We shall see.

To cook a snook at time I have just planted a red chestnut outside the french windows of the Round House. When I talked to my friend Mr Bernhard of Rugby, the nurseryman who owns one of the very best garden centres in the Midlands, I told him with some wistfulness that I would so like to see a red chestnut of my own planting in bloom but supposed I was now to old. He said he could supply me with a well-grown tree which should certainly bear flowers within the next year or so, and this is now firmly staked in the corner of the herbaceous border. It is a tree fully eleven foot tall so I hope to see red blossoms in May, though I may have to wait a year.

The red chestnut is not all that common, nor is it such a good 'doer' as the white and seldom reaches vast proportions. But it is a favourite tree with me, and when I see the chestnut candles lit I know that summer is at its best, or very nearly.

The red may I like also. I have a fine red may by my small pond which I planted some dozen years ago. Each summer it delights me with its rich crimson blooms. I think my love for both the red may and the chestnut stems from childhood memories, when all the world and I were young. I have an affection also for the guelder rose, though this flowers later than the may. As a small boy I thought the white ball-like flowers were edible, and somehow connected them with white bread rolls.

February 11 ———————————————————————

The yew, one of my favourite trees, especially when it is growing wild in the woods as it does in the south country, is apparently our only truly deadly tree, both to humans and animals. I knew that the foliage has been known to kill cattle and horses but did not realize that it was also equally deadly to man, and that if anyone is foolish enough to eat the foliage (not that this is likely unless one is a lunatic) death will come within a few minutes with total heart collapse. Not that this fact

41

lessens my regard for this sombre tree which is so beloved by birds.

Its close foliage seems to defy the worst that winter can do and it is unaffected by the most penetrating frost; it also seems to defy the passage of time and will live longer than any other tree, including the oak. My Irish yews (no less deadly) which I planted in my garden, were a long time in showing growth. Now each year the dark spires rise ever higher. I love the feel of the cold intricate leaves which seem to retain a coolness even in the hot days.

Yet I once knew of a yew which used to grow in a field at Naseby close to the scene of the battlefield, and had never been known to poison stock grazing in that field. Some say that it is only the fallen leaves of the yew which are so deadly to cattle and horses. If this is so it seems strange that even when the juices have gone out of the leaves, they can retain the deadly poison, an alkaloid called *taxine*, which has never been obtained in its pure form.

I remember seeing the ancient yew in Farringdon church-yard in Hampshire (a favourite county for the yew) which was reputed to be over a thousand years old and rivalled the famous Selborne yew. This grows in the churchyard at Selborne and was a favourite tree with W. H. Hudson, who wrote at length about it. The Farringdon yew is of greater girth than the Selborne tree and will no doubt live on for another century or more before time exacts its toll.

The life force in a giant tree always fascinates me, that same life force which is within my own body. It is miraculous when one knows that at one period of time, in its very beginning, that Farringdon yew was a mere tiny seed which you could have held in the hand, smaller far than one's fingernail.

The snowdrops are showing white now under my apple trees and on this mild morning I rejoiced to see the multitudes of white points showing through the grass.

We had a fright two days ago, for the moorhen did not

appear for his usual breakfast and when we found beside the road, not a hundred yards away, the dead body of a moorhen which had been run over, we were sure that it was our well-loved bird. So for two days we mourned and then, when returning from a forest walk yesterday, there was our bird back again on Big Pond and ready for his tea! He was there again this morning and came hurrying down the lawn for breakfast when I called him.

A moorhen runs (or walks) like a mannequin, placing one foot in front of the other, a necessary precaution as their claws are so long. I am hoping that in another week or so he (or she) will find a mate and set up house on Big Pond as of old and raise one or two families.

Despite the soft airs and sunlight and the appearance of snowdrops, I have yet to smell the spring. I refuse to be deceived. There will be another four weeks to that day when I sense the sap is running. Not even the sight and sound of lambs make me think that 'spring has sprung'.

The rooks are wise. Despite these soft warm days the rookeries are still silent and deserted though the old birds sit about by their old nests soon after sunrise. One or two may fuss about with twigs pretending at nest building, but they will do this in the dead of winter should the weather turn mild.

They know as well as I do the time is not yet and that there will be frost and snow to come.

February 12 ───────────────────────────────

This evening, after a day of gentle warmth, the twilight lingered until near six o'clock. I went out into the garden to feed my labrador Polar and was brought up short by hearing, for the first time this year, the warbling of a cock blackbird. This was almost as noticeable as hearing the first chiffchaff, the first of our spring migrants.

I put down Polar's dish and stood quietly by the wall peach tree to savour those so-welcome notes.

The blackbird does not sing as the song-thrush sings; he warbles away for minutes on end. That sweet oboe-like sound, coming to me from across the quiet garden, filled me with delight. It was some time before I could locate him. Then I saw him at the far end of the garden on the weeping willow, a dim, barely seen black shape.

Unlike the more delicate and 'choosey' song-thrush, the blackbird eats a greater variety of food when the weather is hard. Song-thrushes will not eat bread (which anyway is no good for most birds save starlings which seem to be able to digest anything); they will eat fruit, especially apples, and they will eat the chick crumbs I put out for the moorhen. But their diet is more insectivorous, worms and slugs are their staple diet, and some berries.

Already the blackbirds are claiming their territories and at this time of year you can sometimes see as many as a dozen or more cock blackbirds hopping around each other, sometimes indulging in brief sparrings. They flock like blackgame at the 'lek'. Song-thrushes will never do this — they will at times fight but only separate birds, never more than two.

My garden is specially suited to blackbirds. I planted a line of spruce down one side of the garden as well as snowberry, and some yew. Both thrushes and blackbirds build in the spruce every spring but are prone to attacks from marauding jays, and mice sometimes raid the substantial nests.

Listening to my blackbird in the soft interminable twilight made me think of the precise order of nature and the relentless passage of the hours. With what unfailing regularity the seasons pass, what invincible laws govern our spinning space ship, the earth! Yet how could I ever be happy and content in a part of the world where there is no perceptible change between spring, summer, autumn, and winter? It is the gradual approach of each season of the year which gives such pleasure to me, the anticipation of looking for those very first signs, the blackbird's warble, the brimstone butterfly (which I have yet to see this year). But today the first gold club of a crocus showed, one single bloom against the dark earth. I put down its early arrival to the sapping and tunnelling of my wretched mole.

No doubt he dislodged one of the bulbs, heaving it nearer the surface, and that is why it has flowered. I think that February 12 is the earliest date for a yellow crocus in my garden.

Each morning my moorhen awaits his breakfast, sometimes perched on the old sundial on which is inscribed TEMPUS LONGA VITA BREVIS, a warning he ignores. Sometimes he perches on the old stone staddle by Small Pond, sometimes he waits on the lawn, looking up at Angela's bedroom window.

Having had breakfast he spends an idle morning swimming on Big Pond, eating waterweed, or lawn-grazing. At midday he asks for luncheon. Having had this he usually departs, we know not where. If it is across the main road I fear for his life. There are few motorists who will slow down if they see a bird in the road.

The peculiar stillness about these February days continues, no breeze at all to riffle Big Pond. The tall Lombardy poplars rise up motionless against the soft sky. One, I see, has an old thrush's or blackbird's nest half way up, visible now before the leaves come.

It is the same over the quiet fields. You can hear the wheeze of a calling partridge afar off, or the bleat of lambs. All this is part of the turn of the year. Yet the rookeries remain silent and deserted and few old birds are visible. They know the time is not yet.

February 16 ─────────────────────────────

The solemn still weather continues, windless and misty, very like those days we get in early autumn but without any sense of autumn in the air, a sort of waiting for the spring. Walking along a little country road with daughter Angela she put her hand on my arm and said 'a lark'. I could hear nothing, yet that lark was singing vigorously, a song which was at one time one

of my favourites and now, to my sorrow, I cannot hear it! But I could see it, mounting its invisible steps to heaven as though drawn up in jerks like a marionette.

As a boy I was entranced by the rising singing larks. Lying on my back on the Rectory lawn at Lamport I would watch the bird as it left the buttercup meadow, rising in circles, singing as it went. The greatest magic for me was to hear that song dwindling fainter and fainter until the bird was a mere speck high above the earth. I watched the lark this morning until it was lost to sight, but even so Angela, with her young ears, could hear it still. How I envied her!

Then I saw a falling speck. It was dropping like a stone within twenty feet or less of the field when it opened its wings and finished the flight with a long sweeping glide. No wonder the lark has attracted the attention of poets, indeed this habit of soaring high into the sky is shared with no other British bird.

The woodlark will rise some way, so will the tree pipit, and even the little woodwren or woodwarbler will rise upwards in the forest glades and come fluttering down with a leaf-like motion, singing as it falls. But no other bird will climb, singing, into the far upper air. As with many other birds they seem to enjoy life so much more than, say, a crow or any of the hawk tribe. So it is with all our singing birds, those with real powers of song, like the blackbird, song-thrush, the lark family, and the woodland warblers.

I like to see the first warbler hopping in the bud-bursting sallows. He hunts around for insects but at intervals will pause and lift up his head, and with pulsing throat, let fall that tender falling scale of song which is such a delight in the April days. We do not have the woodlark in the dreary Midlands — it is a bird of the south and west, as is the woodwren.

One day stands out in my memory when I was walking alone in a remote Welsh valley. It was a heavenly, early June morning. I was coming down through a ferny wood after a surprising adventure with a buzzard. I had climbed a steep rock and, looking over the edge, found I was staring at the back of a brooding buzzard not three feet below me! I could not believe my eyes. I had a camera with me and was able to photograph her. At the faint click of the camera she twisted her head and looked up at me with her great yellow eye burning with astonishment and horror.

She was gone in a moment. I found there was one unhatched egg in the nest and one white downy monstrosity, a newly hatched baby. I left quickly, for I did not want to keep the hen from her cotton-wool gollywog and it was as I was descending through the oak woods that I heard the strange elfin song of the willow wren. I had not heard this bird before and was for a moment puzzled until I saw it, fluttering round and down, against the background of gold spotted leaves where the bright sunlight was filtering through.

I don't suppose I shall ever forget that divine day. It will be with me as long as memory lasts, there was something quite magical about it. I suppose we get on an average, about three or four such days in early summer each year, when all the foliage is fresh minted. In that Welsh valley there were sheets of golden varnished buttercups which dusted my shoes with yellow pollen as I walked through them, truly a dream of summer. These days occur, sometimes in the first week in June, at the time of the mayfly. They are like jewels. How I pity those who dwell in cities who can never know those fleeting hours of paradise!

February 20 ————————————————————————

There is a war on.

Outside my front gate I have a small lawn and on one side of it a long bed, planted last autumn with a multitude of crocus bulbs. Some weeks before Christmas a mole appeared to have taken up his winter quarters, apparently in the crocus bed which I had top-dressed with a liberal amount of peat. He threw up his heaps of spoil, and his saps and tunnels were visible everywhere under the grass.

48

I have no truck with moles. I have always been able to trap them without any trouble with the usual metal-ring devices. So I set mine close to the crocus bed in a fairly deep run. Next morning I went out to visit my 'trap line' and saw, to my delight, that the two prongs were in a V, a sure sign it was sprung. But when I raised it the jaws were empty. The little gentleman in black velvet had cheated me.

I thought, no matter! this has happened occasionally. I sought another run close to a freshly turned pile of earth. Next morning the trap was sprung again — no Mr Mole! This private war has been going on now for over five weeks, I just cannot catch him!

As an animal the mole has much to recommend it. It is amusing to look at with its almost square black body, the same at both ends like a bolster, so soft and black, and the absurd little pink nose, like that of an anteater, sticking out in front of the square body like a peg. They can swim with great speed, faster than a water vole, for their humanlike hands can act as very serviceable propellers. All moles are 'loners', save in the mating season, when fierce battles take place.

I have them sometimes (to my dismay) on the borders of Big Pond. One day last summer I was horrified to see the Butyl liner near the margin heaving. There was a mole underneath!

His run emerged on the bank. I set a trap there, but failed to catch him. I have a suspicion this is the same mole as he only has to travel some thirty yards to reach my crocus bed. I have examined the trap to see if it has any defect, I have even bought another trap but that has failed me. My only hope is to surprise him heaving the earth; a sharp-tined fork should do the trick. If only I could find at what hour he works, for moles are creatures of method and very punctual.

There has been a plague of them in the Midlands during the present year and last (1979). One farmer I know had been driven to desperate measures in one of his pastures and had to plough it up. As far as I know moles have few enemies. I believe weasels will hunt their burrows and foxes may hunt them, but many say a fox will not eat a mole — mice yes, in abundance, and of course rats — but moles have a peculiar oily smell about them, which the fox find distasteful.

Nobody uses their skins now, for some reason, which is a pity. A moleskin coat was quite luxurious. The old-time keepers often wore waistcoats made of mole skin. As a boy I used to trap them and sell the pelts to relatives for which I was paid ninepence per skin. I skinned them myself, pinning out the skins on a board and rubbing them with saltpetre. Their front labourers' hands are very humanlike, creased in the palm and worn with toil, the nails sharp and long. Moles can also bite if you handle them incautiously.

I remember very vividly an incident when I was about seven, sitting with our governess, under the big cedar tree at my old home one hot summer afternoon. Not far off was a very large holly tree and opposite to it, across the driveway, a holly bush.

I noticed a mole hurrying across from one tree to the bush. It was doing this at intervals of about seven minutes or so. What work it was engaged upon I could not imagine, but I was determined to capture it. So I waited quietly behind the bole of the big holly and, sure enough, out came a pink peg snout and a black velvet body. It was halfway over the path when I fell upon it, clutching it behind the head. But its small pink snout darted sideways and it bit me on the finger. I dropped it with a yell, it vanished under the smaller holly. A tiny incident, yet the picture has remained in my brain for sixty-eight years. I can remember the sunlight dappling the path, the smell of the great cedar, and the dried skeletons of the holly leaves under which my prize vanished.

What is it in the brain which retains these pictures when we know every atom in our bodies has been changed a hundred times?

I sense a magic at this time of the year when the smell of winter is still evident at evening, when the snow lies in shady nooks and corners, and the light is long a-dying at close of day. It takes me back to my childhood days in the old Rectory garden with its dark holly shrubberies, the great cedar, the snow lying in ribs on the Rectory paddock where our old gardener Gunn grazed the family geese.

For now, in these late evenings, there is a new smell at twilight. It has a distinctly winter tang, but there is something else. Can it be the stirring of the sap, the movement under the tangled grass of the quiet fields?

In those far-off twilights of childhood I remember standing under the old cedar and hearing, afar off, the long drawn 'Hoo! (interval) Hoo!' of the Little Lilford owls which nested freely all around the meadows, mostly in the pollarded ashes. It was a noise quite unlike the hoot of an owl, it was one single melancholy note, long drawn out, the mating call of the Lilford owl. There would be snowdrops, white spears in the Nut Walk and the closed-up golden clubs of the first crocus shut against the evening chill.

Those are the moments of childhood which most of us leave behind when we are adult but which, I must confess, still linger with me.

There was something quite magical to that small boy looking out across the valley (one of the most beautiful views in the whole county of Northamptonshire); seeing the night come close over the fields and fishponds; to smell, so keenly, the scent of the damp shrubberies; and see the snow drifts, no longer white, but blue in the dusk. I knew that summer was coming, with all its joys, that behind me in the house fires and lamps were lit — a different, secure, unexciting world awaiting me. But here, in the shadowy garden, under that noble cedar, which still stands (as does the big holly where I nearly caught my mole), I was aware of a magical world of the wild where the night animals were awakening: the fox in the wood, the owls in the old church tower where my father preached each Sunday — a far from secure world, where, like the jungle, one must die that another might live.

Some will be thinking 'that's a sign of age , harking back to boyhood days'. Not at all. I have always looked back and remembered and always will. We can only recollect brief moments of time, sometimes silly, inconsequential things, but with me it is nearly always something to do with the open air, a moment of time which when we experienced it made no sharp impression, yet afterwards remained, mysteriously, for a lifetime.

So now, with the light still lingering in the western sky long after winter 'tea-time', I can stand in my garden and sniff the coming spring, listen to the first low fluting of the cock blackbirds, upon which I remark every year, and recapture my childhood.

Does the poor town or city captive sense this magic of the open air? Perhaps he may, in the large parks such as Richmond, and even Hyde Park, though when I was a student in London I found no magic there, only an almost unbearable yearning for the woods and fields of home.

Small children of both sexes, walking by the Serpentine, perhaps, on one of these March evenings, may sense something of what I used to feel in that old Rectory garden over seventy years ago. I hope they do, even though it may be but a feeble echo of the distant countryside, with its fields, woods, and rivers.

Certainly the ducks on the Serpentine feel this magic, and the nightly 'Quar! Quar!' of the uneasy mallard drakes is not entirely drowned by the continuous dull roar of traffic, where the teeming city glows behind a grill of still naked trees in Park Lane and Kensington.

Numbers of these city mallards flight out like their country cousins, many to the lower reaches of the Thames where rich pickings may be found, and even to the countryside outside the suburbs. Yet, like the starling flocks, they enjoy city life.

The love that the starlings have for the centre of the big cities shows what gregarious creatures they are, the more the merrier. The grimy and sooty cornices and mouldings of the great Victorian buildings are preferable to distant cold thickets of thorn far out in the sleeping countryside.

There are bright lights and noise and above all, warmth.

As evening closes the flocks come in like locust swarms from all sides, wheeling against the sunset sky in aerial manoeuvres with the precision of Guardsmen at drill. When at last these exercises are completed they drop down to the grimy ledges, jostling one another for a place, singing and chattering with a gale of noise that can be heard above the roar of traffic.

I remember some years ago when I had to give a broadcast for the BBC in Birmingham (on Christmas Eve of all times!) I witnessed the descent of the starling flock and marvelled at the noise they made. It is the same in all our big cities, London, Birmingham, Liverpool and Newcastle.

As the hours pass and midnight draws near, the singing and babel of voices die. Soon all are silent with intucked heads, save for an occasional squeal or chatter. Within those thousands of craniums what dreams? Dreams of far countries where many have been born, away in northern Europe? Dreams of English fields? Or far-off nesting holes?

Even as the restless hum of the city dies, so does the chattering throng seek silence and sleep until the East pales with a new day and flock after flock depart once more for the open country. The birds of the countryside regard mankind with well-merited suspicion and fear, but to the starlings man is a friend, providing warmth and noise, two ingredients which contribute much to the enjoyment of their brief lives.

February 24 _____

On February 11 I wrote in the *Shooting Times* of the poisonous prospectus of the yew. Today I had a letter from that tree expert, Arthur Cadman, who once looked after the New Forest and who latterly was a wildfowling crony of mine.

He tells me that the deer in the New Forest — where there are plenty of yew trees (as there are in many of the Hampshire woods) sometimes ate the foliage of the tree, but took no harm as long as they did not eat a large quantity of the leaves. But cattle had been found dead near yews and so had the occasional deer, where the animal had eaten the *dead* foliage which seems to contain the poison in a more lethal dose. In the New Forest, when the snow is deep, no doubt the deer are ravenous and will eat yew which they would avoid at other times.

I have also received other letters — one from a retired Army Colonel who had lost a horse through eating yew, and one from a vet who sent me numerous notes on the subject.

I have not been back to the New Forest for thirty years, but my memories of it are still with me, for I went in the spring time just when the primroses were out and the oaks were showing green.

I stayed in a millhouse near Hatchet Pond, and what wonderful days those were — wandering in the green ridings searching for adders, which have always had a fearful fascination for me. That April the weather was as warm as June but I saw no adders save a dead one, though was rewarded by identifying a smooth snake — a much more uncommon customer.

Somehow, coming upon an ancient yew in the forest gives one a strange feeling of medieval times. The tree is connected in the mind with the 'running of the deer', and at that comparatively leafless time of the year — mid-April — before the oaks are in full leaf, to come upon a dark yew or ancient holly clump makes a delightful contrast.

The strengthening sun, casting an intricate web of shadows on the forest floor, where last November's oak leaves still lie, makes a deeper shadow on the ground.

In my garden I have planted two Irish yews between two ponds and between them a golden elm — an uncommon tree not often seen in gardens. In summer the leaves of the golden elm make a wonderful contrast to the sombre spires of the Irish yews and the tree retains that golden colour right through until the autumn. I wonder that more people do not plant this delightful and most decorative tree. It does not grow to a great size like the common elm, and does well in suburban gardens. Whether it is affected by elm disease

54

I do not know. As it is a relative it may be susceptible.

The term 'golden' is not an exact description of the colour. It has, to my mind, a greater resemblance to the leaf of the hedge maple in autumn — a delightful soft amber yellow.

A day or so ago the sun shone like mid-May. The little field lambs rejoiced and ran races, and bees — the first honey bees of the year — were visiting the opening crocus buds, but now winter has returned, a nasty little east wind stirs the dead hemlock rods in the hedgerow and a mist cloaks the forest.

That is why I dislike February, it is the most treacherous of all months. I saw a solitary rook perched on the highest twig of an ash in the wood, regarding with evident disfavour this dreary day. His shoulders were hunched and he supported his breast-bone on the twig, the picture of dejection.

These wise birds know the weather-to-be better than any weather forecaster. The old nests still remain unvisited in the rookeries as the bare twigs hiss and sway in the cruel east wind.

I could not help wondering what was passing through that birdy mind as he sat so high on that bleak, misty ash tree. Perhaps he was lovesick and his lady-love had deserted him — one does not often see a solitary rook, for they love each other's company. Not far off, another ash tree was crowded with jackdaws — they too had little to say but sat about disconsolately like the lone rook.

I like both species and associate them with spacious parklands and great estates, for the jackdaws love the old oaks, stag headed and full of breeding holes. On all ancient parklands such trees are to be found. The noise of a rookery in spring is as evocative as the voice of the cuckoo which heralds summer days. The female rooks sit upon their nests and wave their wings, as the young ones will soon do, when the male arrives with his pouch full of grubs. The hideous practice of shooting the perchers in May — just before they leave the nest — is still continued in some parts of the country, but I deplore it.

Like many other of our birds, the rook is far less numerous than formerly due to the farmers' sprays. If some farmers had their way they would exterminate every bird on their farms. One of my greatest friends is a farmer but he is a conservationist, even setting aside and planting a piece of land with weeds and bushes to attract birds and butterflies. He is an exception.

The moorhen, whom I have named Pruick! from his call note, has been with us for the last few days of sun but now that the grim grey weather rules once more he has departed. It is a mystery where he goes to, for we have never seen him fly directly out of the garden.

Perhaps he has a mate up the brook and divides his time between her and me.

March 1 _____

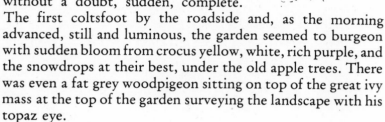

February gone (and a leap year
February, too!) Today it was as if
the year turned a page — spring
without a doubt, sudden, complete.
The first coltsfoot by the roadside and, as the morning
advanced, still and luminous, the garden seemed to burgeon
with sudden bloom from crocus yellow, white, rich purple, and
the snowdrops at their best, under the old apple trees. There
was even a fat grey woodpigeon sitting on top of the great ivy
mass at the top of the garden surveying the landscape with his
topaz eye.

When I was young I would have reached for my rifle —
now I rejoiced to welcome him to my little garden, for I love
the soothing voice of the ring dove — so different from the
mourning of the collared doves which infest the place.

And later at twilight all the cock blackbirds began to
warble. High over the Douglas firs which fringe my garden
wall I heard the faint 'crank crank' of a passing heron. I could
just make out his large flapping wings, moving with majesty,
oaring himself along as a man rows a boat on a quiet pool,
across the dim sky.

Why did he call thus? A solitary traveller, bound for a
field pond high on the lonely hill which years before the farmer
stocked with carp, carp from my own lake at the Lodge before
we moved to my present home. Just why did he call as he
passed over the darkening countryside, was it pleasure at the
feel of spring, at the lengthening twilight? He had no companion that I could see.

Often when two herons are voyaging they call to each
other. The repeated sound 'Frank! Frank!', harsh but far-
reaching, had a wild flavour, I heard it die away northwards.

What was going on in that strange, almost serpentine,

cranium? His long legs, locked together behind him by the hind claws (a necessary action when in flight otherwise they would be flying all ways with the rhythmic exertions of his big wings), his spear bill cleaving the soft evening air, and those large rounded vanes which beat the air with slow and regular motion — I think he was enjoying this evening hour — his mind was busy with the deserted farm pond on the hill top where man seldom came, and all the fat carp that would be his by moonrise. And there he would fish under the moon, no doubt until the dawn, whilst I was tucked up asleep like a beetle under a stone.

For the first time also today I noticed the rooks about the oak tops busy with their first frail foundations of their nests. How delicate and sure must those twigs be interlaced among the bare mist of twigs!

March 8 _____

After three days of divine spring weather with the fish beginning to move in Big Pond, and all the crocuses ablaze, winter has returned with cold winds. Today — rain, rain, rain from a glowering putty-coloured sky.

How can I write on such a bleak day as this? Low clouds mean a lowness of spirit — I am certain that when the barometer is low so does one's sense of wellbeing fall. Yet I have just been looking at the rookery in the next village — the old birds fussing with their nests, nests which a week ago were not visible. Now some are substantial, and building goes on apace. What intrigued me was a love-sick couple of birds perched high on their twiggy castle turret pressed together oblivious of the slanting rods of cold rain. Both faced the west wind, but they seemed happy in each other's company, newly weds perhaps, and with a lifetime before them if the fates are kind.

They seemed to care not one jot for the wet west wind which rocked the twigs around them, to be next to one's beloved was all that mattered. I rejoiced in their simple loving.

From their high vantage point they could survey the whole village spread out below them, the old grey church tower, the thatched cottages and trashy modern bungalows, and beyond the village the quiet fields, so green now after the warm spring days.

Rooks are supposed to mate for life, as do many other birds. They are perhaps the most British of all our wild birds and I love them.

At last there is dog's mercury up in Bullocks Wood, I saw it yesterday for the first time. Only a week or so ago the woodland floor was bare, strewn with last November's oak leaves, now a green carpet is shooting up everywhere, hiding the russets and buffs of the woodland floor, with them also the bluebell shoots. In another eight weeks the oaks in Bullocks Wood will stand with their feet in a sea of blue and white, for the wild garlic grows there too, making a rare contrast to the bluebells. Dog's mercury tells of the age of the woodland. At one period Bullocks Wood was part of the Forest of Rockingham, as are all the woods around my house.

Like the yew it is a poisonous plant, cattle avoid eating it, nor will dogs touch it.

Dog's mercury is believed to have been used by the ancients for medicinal purposes, but why it is called dog's mercury is obscure, unless it was supposed to be good dog medicine. In some of the Midland woods it forms a thick green carpet. I fancy it dislikes sunlight for one never finds it out in the open; like the bluebell it prefers dappled shade.

Despite the recent divine days of warm sun (even my infant purple emperor larvae were showing signs of stirring — raising their little horns expectantly), no brimstone butterfly went plodding down the windless woodsides, they are still in hibernation among the ivy leaves on the woodland oaks. Marvellously camouflaged they are too among the shiny veined leaves; even the shape of their wings, quite different from those of any other of our British butterflies, resembles the points of the ivy leaf.

Though there is as yet no signs of green buds on the

roadside hedges there is one stretch of hawthorn hedge outside the steel town of Corby (of all places!) which shows green before any other I know. When I passed that way a week ago some of the lower branches were powdered with green. This hedge faces south so gets all the sun there is, but is unprotected on the north side, so it is a puzzle why it should be the first to welcome the spring.

My pet bullfinches dearly love to eat the tiny green opening buds of the hawthorn and, later, I give them a spray of apple blossom which they like, not the fully opened flowers but the tight pink buds. Sparrows will also eat the buds of apple but in a half-hearted manner.

A pair of bullies will give your fruit buds a thorough going-over about early May and if not discouraged will rob you of fruit later on; no British bird is so damaging to our orchards. Yet how could anyone destroy this lovely British finch? It is a lover of the woodlands as much as the woodpigeon and woodcock, the blackcap and garden warbler.

Thinking again on birds in wet weather, I suppose most birds and animals (apart from wildfowl and water-loving creatures like the otter and vole) dislike driving rain. A steady rain will soon empty your garden of birds, they retire to the bushes and hedgerows for shelter. Only the mistle-thrush or 'stormcock' as the country people call it (horse-thrush is another local name) will sing in wind and rain. How sad it is that mistle-thrushes are now so uncommon in the Midland countryside! The last one I heard singing was in the middle of Kettering, in a suburban garden!

These big bold birds were great favourites of mine, for in the garden of my birth place they built every year with unfailing regularity on the knuckle of an ancient yew. Every April they built there, and each year I climbed to the big mossy nest to admire the unthrushlike eggs with their violet and grey streaks and rich marblings of Vandyck brown.

The song too is most attractive, again unlike that of the song-thrush, and more akin to the ring ousel's song or the blackbird's. It is a wild song which carries a great distance, possibly helped by the high perch of the chorister for they invariably seek out the highest twig in the eye of the wind. It is an early songster too; they sing in January when the weather is mild which a blackbird will never do.

W. H. Hudson speaks of them roving the downs after snails at summer's end and indeed they are not stay-at-home garden birds but travel far when breeding chores are over. Many of our Midland mistle-thrushes go south in August and September and do not return until winter's end.

Every evening now a pair of portly woodpigeons continue to visit the great ivy tree at the top of my garden. They eat the berries, and I think they hope to build there. I hope they do so for, strange as it may sound, the woodpigeon is by no means common these days in Northamptonshire. The reason is hard to find unless the farmers have access to some secret weapon dreamt up by the boffin boys.

It may be that woodpigeons have changed their habits and do not frequent the grass fields as they used to do when I was a boy. They go for the fields of rape which now seem so popular as a crop. Now in most rape fields the farmers have their scare guns which bang away all through the daylight hours, and in some cases nights as well, and then the regular explosions can be a real menace to the country dweller, keeping him awake, though to leave a 'banger' on all night is illegal. It is one more aggravating sound now in the farming areas; the 'quiet fields' are quiet no longer where rape is grown.

Man is becoming an increasingly noisy animal with his motor-car, tractor and aeroplane. Sometimes, however, the bumbling sound of a distant plane can be sleep inducing.

Last summer, when out in the middle of the vast Rutland water on a day of heat and millpond conditions, I lay in the bottom of the boat and was lulled to sleep by the far-off rumblings of passing planes. Conditions were hopeless for fishing. Not a 'ring of bright water' disturbed that vast inland sea and all fishermen like myself were asleep on the bottom boards.

These idle hours of a summer's day are not unpleasant.

Occasionally the lap-lap of ripples clucks under your moored craft, high up in the blue sky under a brazen sun you can watch the swifts soaring and wheeling, and even the hunting instinct of the male animal is in abeyance.

March 9

The cruel north-east wind continues, it sings in the intricate web of bare hedgerow twigs, it sets the firs tossing and the tops of the tall elms, those as yet free of the dread disease.

This morning I watched the rooks again; they were quite unperturbed by the return of winter, and more and more nests were being built. I have seen no fieldfares this year in any numbers, just the odd one or two — redwings being more plentiful — but nothing like the numbers I remember as a boy. In winter time the pastures were full of the fieldfare flocks, they were as numerous as woodpigeons.

I always think the fieldfare the most handsome of all the thrush family, with his soft grey rump, dark tail, chestnut mantle and grey head, and the breast is as handsomely striped as a hawk's egg, with bold streaks and blotches of Vandyck brown.

When my brother was at school in Worcestershire he always maintained he came upon a small colony of fieldfares nesting in a fir wood near Bromsgrove. He was an observant ornithologist and egg-collector and he took one of the fieldfares' eggs for his collection.

The redwing occasionally breeds in Scotland and it is suspected that the fieldfare does also on occasion. It is a true bird of the 'quiet fields' and is well named.

In winter when the weather is icy and snow covers the fields it will roost in long tussocks of grass. I remember disturbing hundreds out of a rough tussock margin to the Rugby reservoir at Stanford-on-Avon. On that snowy twilight I remember I also put up an old dog fox out of the same dead grass, no doubt he was about to make a meal out of the roosting birds.

March 10

The peewits were calling over the sunny ploughlands this morning, heard afar, the thin 'week a week, two bullocks a week' came faintly on the soft west wind, true voice of spring! It is the first time this year I have heard that sound, almost as important to me as the liquid chuckle of the first swallow or falling scale of the willow warbler.

On a southern hedge beside the road which had been clipped close by the machine (truly laid hedges are becoming few and far between as the old art of hedge-laying dies with the older men), each twig had the pale green point of the coming buds.

Down in the quiet fields the brook flashed in the sun, and some portly old mother sheep were suckling their tottering lambs. The wandering brook which traverses the gentle folds of the field feeds a newly made pond in a corner of the meadow where some ancient hawthorn trees grow.

Upon its bright expanse sat three wild mallard, with another on the bank surveying the brave morning. The wary fowl had seen us as soon as we topped the rise in the road and though they were fully two hundred yards distant they took quacking wing.

Both geese and ducks can see great distances, so can the pheasant. Yet later today when we spied the fowl on the Eye Brook reservoir, a pack of about fifty wigeon were resting on the short grass not fifty yards from the road where a dozen bird-watchers were training their glasses on them.

Through my binoculars I could bring them within touching distance. What a beautiful thing is the wigeon drake with his jet black bottom set off with white, the sulphur caste mark on his chestnut head and the white on the wing the same as the

63

chaffinch! Some were asleep with intucked bills, but most were upending in the sunlit water.

The reservoir being so full, the shore was not more than thirty yards from the road, the fullest I have seen it. The water had even reached the chestnut tree where in the summer heats we sometimes eat our luncheon in its shade, then we have to plod up a hundred yards of turf to reach it. I have caught some fine trout opposite this tree, for the bay is a favourite one with me.

For the trim wigeon, these last few weeks of March are the end of the holidays. Soon they will be dispersing, some to the Highlands of Scotland and others, the bulk of them overseas, each to their breeding stations. By April's end these green shores of the reservoir will be deserted save for teal and mallard and the ever-present coots and herons.

Looking across the expanse of shining water to the far shore where a group of willows glowed orange, I remembered one day of tropical heat when a doctor friend and I were becalmed on the windless water with every fish asleep and drowsing, the worst conditions for fishing.

As I reclined on the bottom boards with a wet handkerchief over my brow (the cool drips running deliciously into my eyes) I observed a strange cleaving ripple some thirty yards distant. Something was swimming just under the surface, leaving a V wake. It was progressing at rowing pace. This needed prompt investigation. I set my electric motor at low speed and set off in pursuit.

As we got nearer, silently gliding, leaving behind us a similar V-shaped wake, I saw a humped scaled back which now and again broke surface. Could it be a giant trout? When we came within a few feet of the fish, we saw it was a gigantic carp which must have weighed well into double figures. It was nosing along like a cruising whale. When we were almost upon it it dived, leaving a swirl in the water. We did not see it again.

On another occasion, when fishing under similar conditions, I saw a fine tench which must have weighed well over five pounds just under our keel. Most reservoirs hold coarse

fish and it is a puzzle to know how they get into reservoirs — probably they are introduced by fishermen on the sly.

Certainly no carp or tench were put into the Eye Brook when it was stocked. Roach and pike were often in the feeding brooks before the reservoir was constructed. I once found a four-inch pike up a little side stream way out in the fields.

At this time of mid-March it is strange to look back on the days of high summer when the weather is hot and no breeze ruffles the surface of these inland seas.

On either hand the fields of rape make a false sunlight on the swelling hills, swifts arrow overhead, some rushing past the anchored boat, their dusky wings driving them with tremendous speed so you can hear the rush of air in their curved vanes. The floorboards in the boat are almost too hot to touch and the chance of a rise is negligible. You might as well give it up and go to sleep.

Yet I recall one such occasion, when a summer sun burned in a cloudless sky, when my rod was almost catapulted out of the boat by a trout which had come up under the keel, spied my dangling fly, and departed at speed. In an instant all was frantic activity. I grabbed the butt and played the fish, a rainbow of about two pounds' weight.

When the level of the reservoir drops in a dry summer, a vast margin of cracked earth remains, strewn with empty mussel shells and moisture-starved weeds, rafts of water plantain with its pink flowers, which lie like winkles on seaside rocks praying for the turn of the tide.

This sun-baked desert gives off a strange, wild, minty aroma almost like the smell of sea-weed. The beachcomber may find on these barren margins old discarded nylon casts, beer tops, sometimes coins, once even a 'priest', the small wooden club used for despatching fish, no doubt dropped over the side of the boat in some distant frantic fishy encounter.

Even in the boat itself can be discovered lost flies and hooks.

Once I found, fixed in a crevice on the bottom boards, a tattered, worn fly which I put on my cast, having tried a selection of flies in my book without any success. Immediately I hooked a fine trout with this wretched apology of a lure. I did well with it in later days and eventually lost it in a big fish, to my great tribulation.

March 11 ────────────────────────────

I have been greatly moved by Attenborough's TV series *Life on Earth*. This magnificent series somehow made me realize that, as we grow older, time becomes of supreme importance, at least it does for me.

The very miracle of being alive is intensified. In youth we do not give the passing minutes a single thought. I feel now that not a second must be wasted, even to sleep seems a wicked waste! The steady rhythm of days and seasons, the joy I find in the pattern and colour of the most humble wayside weed, the feel and smell of the winds of spring, the beauty of the natural world, how can I describe my delight?

Surely the city dweller cannot really *live*? I know that in probably less than a dozen years the frail envelope which now encloses me will be of no more import than a stick or stone. Yet being part of nature, even for so brief a moment, has been for me supremely worthwhile. I would not have missed this experience, and am filled with a great thankfulness that I have been able to be part of nature's scheme, the same forces which make the acorn grow into a great oak (I am sure trees enjoy life and rejoice in the feel of the sun on their leaves and the gentle caress of summer rain). How can anyone be miserable if one has health and strength? Yet what a mess some of us make of life, squandering the passing seconds! What importance we attach to trivial things; how I echo W. H. Hudson's words, 'It has been better to have lived than never to have lived at all'!

By what incalculable billion-to-one chance have I been able to have this experience? Not only to exist on this planet (the only one as far as we know which sustains life) but to be a man and not a silver fish, spider, sea urchin, or humble microbe.

67

The time is coming so rapidly when man and womankind will have many more hours of leisure from work. The beauty of the countryside is there to be enjoyed unless we destroy it and ourselves in one insane atomic explosion. Through avarice and selfishness we may indeed destroy mankind and, with ourselves, many of the creatures who share this planet with us. But nature will in time recover, scarred and poisoned no doubt for some centuries, but then a different life cycle would begin again, for this globe can sustain life for many millions of years to come before it, too, ceases to be.

Having lived once, is it not just possible that we shall live again? I have hope when I see one of my lovely purple emperor chrysalids split and the finished article emerge, to leave that frail empty skin, discarded rubbish, which my own body will one day become.

All these thoughts passed through my mind as I sat this morning on the old stone seat by Big Pond. Crude philosophy? Maybe, so be it. The sun shone warmly on the water where the fresh green sword blades of wild iris are beginning to pierce the sodden ruin of last year's growth.

Bees were investigating the purple and white crocuses round the base of the old apple trees and the water of Big Pond gave off that faint aroma of fish, a smell you never get in a fishless water. Somewhere in the ochre depths a big carp swims, a fish of over six pounds in weight, a coy creature who only shows himself on summer evenings when, in a fit of exuberance, he leaps clear of the water presenting a sudden quite astonishing vision of gold mail.

He once erupted underneath a swimming moorhen which fled screaming hysterically to the bank. There are other fish in the pond but these are more visible, coming for their nightly feed of bread. Then the still water becomes alive with their splashing curving bodies.

The big carp has a history. About thirty years ago, when I lived at Woodford Lodge, I stocked the lovely lake there one November afternoon with fish brought in a car from London, as described in my memoirs *A Child Alone*. When some sixteen years later I left the Lodge, the lake was full of large carp and a friend brought me one for my present Big Pond together with two smaller ones. In the hard winter of 1978/79 one died in the ice but the others survived.

The golden orfe in my small pond weighs around three pounds and is at least thirty years old. Its companion was devoured by a poaching heron under the moon.

March 14

I was interested to read the other day that fish feel pain. How this was proved I do not know. I have recently read an account of a carp which was caught no less than eight times in succession in a single day. There was no doubt about its being the same fish as it had an identifying mark on its gill cover. This certainly suggests that fish do not feel great discomfort when hooked in the mouth, though a 'live' bait for pike, which is hooked in the body as well as the mouth, may be a different matter.

The mouths of coarse and game fish are mostly gristle and this may account for the carp coming eight times to the bait. Today I was again amazed to see two 'coarse' fishermen sitting under their umbrellas on the banks of the Nene. This time they were after eels, not pike. The rain was pelting down, driven by an icy north-westerly wind, indeed it continued thus all day without lifting. Yet these hardy souls fished on, determined to stick it out. What dedication! What hardihood!

Well, I suppose that is preferable to slaving away at a factory bench all day long.

I have odd views about fishing, as perhaps I have on shooting. When I fish it is primarily to either catch a 'specimen', that is a really big fish, whether carp or trout, and secondly, I like to eat what I catch just as I like to eat what I shoot.

Yet the majority of coarse fishermen *never* eat what they

catch. The small fish which come to bank are placed in a keep-net sunk in the water which, on a successful day, must resemble the Black Hole of Calcutta with thirty or forty fish all crowded together unable to get enough oxygen. The prime target seems to be to catch as many as you can. By the day's end many of the inmates of the keep-net will have died.

Perch from a clean river or gravel pool are excellent on the table, so are gudgeon, carp, and tench. The latter have quite a golden flesh but they must come from clean water. As for freshwater eeels I like them almost as much as fresh salmon, especially when smoked. I have one of the 'Abu' fish smokers and on this I put trout and even fresh herrings when I can get them.

I visited the rookery at Twywell, the little village near my home, this morning and saw the rooks busier than ever and still the same pair(?) of love birds sitting side by side on a branch. Meeting an old friend, George Childs, in the village street he told me that his bedroom window overlooks the rookery (lucky man!). He said the old birds were busy at five o'clock this morning when it was barely light.

The peculiar caw, the spring caw, of the busy rooks can be heard all over the village, a wonderfully evocative sound for me as years ago I lived close to a rookery.

March 16

I 'put the clocks on' last night. It brought summer no nearer, quite the reverse. I awoke to another cheerless day with a cold east wind and a sky of uniform grey; it was impossible to guess whether the sun was in the sky at any time during the day. I chose this melancholy afternoon to make an expedition into the County of Huntingdon to sample its strange quality.

A mist veiled the far distances and those huge fields, as big as Fenland fields, stretched away to the horizon. No hedges lined the sides of the bye roads, deep ditches only, filled with water, which reflected in low key the sad sky. All along the sides of the dykes grew dead ragged weeds and teazles, many undamaged by the winter frosts and storms.

What fascinated me, I might say, with an awful fascination, were those vast fields, all either ploughland, green rape, or springing winter wheat. In the centre of these rape fields were fortresses of straw bales, no doubt ambuscades for gunners to keep the pigeons from the crop. Yet we saw not a single woodpigeon all afternoon. Sometimes, far in the centre of these plains, was a solitary tree, an oak or elm, and sometimes a small pond ringed round with bird-sown willows, oaks and ashes.

The farmhouses too seemed grimly functional, standing alone far from the road, many with not even a planted tree to keep off the east wind. What hardy folk these Huntingdonshire farmers must be! What a drear and lonely life for their women!

One can feel the nearness of the fens away to the east, yet many of these fields are far from flat, many are gentle swelling hills with perhaps a ragged coppice of diseased elms lining the boundaries, many already bereft of bark, naked and forlorn.

No birds seemed to haunt that land, no peewits or starlings, not even a hare. Away from the main Cambridge-Kettering road all the metal signposts had been wrecked by vandals, broken off short near the centre post. What mindless destruction! Perhaps the melancholy winter landscape had got the better of the local youth, far from the delights of town and 'discos', those hotbeds of juvenile mischief.

One brighter thing, however, we saw as we turned homewards past a wood delightfully named Salome Wood. Clusters of primroses were already opening on the banks of a drainage ditch in which grew clumps of 'pussy willow' wands studded with silver pearly buttons.

No doubt at one time Salome Wood was composed of oaks, now it is of dense firs planted very close together, a solid block of conifer.

A few white pigeon fluffs were blowing in the grass, and orange cartridge cases lay around which suggested Salome

71

Wood was a pigeon roost. There are no more trees anywhere near it, the huge fields stretch away on either hand; fields which to my mind are quite different from my own 'quiet fields' of grass where lambs run and the boundary hedges are tall century-old hawthorns. It was quite a relief to get back to the homely meadows and woods of home. Yet, and yet, there is something fascinating about that county. It is preferable to the fens, yet in a sense more lonely and remote, and the villages, mere hamlets in many cases, few and far between and not one great wooded estate to be seen.

March 17 ——————————————————————————————

I have an obsession for ponds. I have written about them so much, I do so again. Unfortunately the field-pond (there used to be one in most Midland pastures) have been done away with, yet a few remain, remote and undrained. I spied one today on a walk and climbed the gate in the hedge to investigate.

It lay some five hundred yards from the road and was hedged round completely with willows, oaks, and ashes. It was little larger than my Big Pond in my garden, some forty yards across, maybe, and was almost circular save for a small open 'beach' on the southern side. At one time it had a post-and-rail fence around the 'cattle drink' but this had gone, save for two posts and a rail slanting into the water, originally put there to prevent the cattle getting bogged. There was a dense hawthorn tree close to the margin which spread over the water. I made a mental note to visit again in late May when the hawthorn flowers were out, for I was seeing the pond now in its worse aspect, the day was bitter, the sky a sullen grey, no birds were visible on the big ivy clad oak.

But there was a brave pallisade of green sedge blades at one end. Widening rings in the water told of the present tenants, moorhens, whose private estate this was, one to be handed down to generations of moorhens, for they guard their inheritance with jealousy.

There was some underwater green weed, possibly crow-foot or water forget-me-not, and a few spear-shaped leaves of a bronze hue, water plantain no doubt. Drowned oak leaves were visible in the shadows, but by the cattle drink the pond bottom slid away into peat-brown darkness; probably it was several feet deep at that spot.

What a secret place was this little pond, set away in the quiet fields! The sky, being a November grey, was echoed one tone darker on the surface, almost a purplish colour. Last autumn's weeds, nettle stalks, hemlock and broome grass choked one bank, ashy white and brittle, the dead grass arching over, their tips touching the water forming a hiding place for voles and waterhens and perhaps a skulking pheasant, for pheasants have a liking for such places, especially in autumn when the acorns are ripe.

I was fascinated by the way the crowding bird-sown trees had their pale robust roots in the water resembling weathered jetty piles. From the big willow (whose hollowed trunk no doubt was tenanted by owls) the roots were visible, in a wide fibrous shelf of pink tendrils feeling down into the brown depths like the trailing tentacles of jelly-fish, beautiful vivid rootlets, some as red as rubies. The willow is a thirsty tree and drinks deep.

There was a pale mark on the trunk of a giant ash which showed the winter high-water mark. Day after day, month after month, no one goes near that pond save perhaps an exploring village boy who comes to raid the moorhens' eggs in April holidays. It is almost like a Kopje on an African Veldt for all around are flat fields of pasture and plough, as far as the eye could see.

There must be many little wild people whose house it is, under those sturdy pale roots, in the thicket of hawthorn, in the jungle of rushes. Here the grey jug-like woodpigeons would come to dip their soft bills deep in the midday heats. The wild pigeon drinks like a cow or horse, it never sips like other birds.

In these very early summer mornings when the white

73

petals of the hawthorn lie in rafts of snow on the surface of the water and the larks sing over the springing wheat the cuckoos come to this oasis, perching on the topmost branches of the old oak, monotonously calling that bell-like sound as a challenge to other cuckoos over the quiet fields.

Sometimes the repeated call will continue for forty times or more, the throat swelling like a ball with each 'cuckoo'.

Before even the farmer is awake, before the workers set out for the fields, this is a moment of paradise and true loveliness of the world, when the hares can play in the dew-wet wheat and the partridge stretches a wing over an extended claw in a sense of lazy security.

In the old days, even as late as the mid-twenties of this century, the call of the corncrake was a summer sound now stilled forever by the march of 'progress'. I saw and heard the last one in the summer of 1935.

The hares visit it, not for drink but for the secret shelter, the partridges run about like clockwork toys calling 'keeze, keeze' on winter evenings, and the jays, those beautiful blue-winged cheeky rascals, come for the acorns when they are ripe in the gold October days, so do the blue-black sheeny rooks.

The cruel east winds may come tearing across the flat featureless fields, hissing in the thorns, tossing the crooked oak twigs, whirling the russet lower leaves, but barely a ripple disturbs the sleeping surface of the water.

Remote field ponds are always visited towards the end of winter by the wild mallards. They like the peace and sense of security. When the first primroses show their pale yellow clumps along the southern hedge-side, they spend their days there and often nest in the surrounding herbage. Sometimes they will nest quite a distance from the pond in a hedgerow. When the ducklings hatch, the duck will lead them to the pond, a perilous journey because of the vicious carrion crows. Rats are their worst enemies, that is why the mallards prefer the distant hedge for nesting.

Another pond I know, again in a remote pasture, though without surrounding trees, is notable for its uncommon water plants, bog bean and bladderwort. The latter grows plentifully in some of the Norfolk dykes but is rare in Northamptonshire.

The pond is a picture in summer when the bladderworts are in flower, one end of the pond is a forest of upright purple stalks bearing the strange orange flowers. I have attempted to introduce it to Big Pond but it never lives long, I think the moorhens pull it to pieces.

The bog bean, however, flourishes where the stream enters and, despite the attentions of the waterfowl which pull it about, it manages to bloom in season. The plants came from a Welsh bog, I collected them on one of my expeditions to Wales when I roved the country with my van.

I rashly introduced the American duck weed to Big Pond and since my moorhens have gone elsewhere I have a job to keep it in check. If I did not dredge it out every month it would cover the water from end to end. The moorhens loved to eat it and when they were in residence confined it to the edges. Another plant, the beautiful flowering rush, survived for a season or two but again the moorhens killed it, as they did all my waterlillies which at one time made a brave show.

There is another uncommon rush which I remember from boyhood days, the orange-scented rush. This grew in a little duck pond at the bottom of the Rectory meadow. I have never found it anywhere else. If the juicy blades were crushed between the fingers the scent of oranges was strong. The bladderwort pond is in a flowery meadow near the river Nene, a meadow which is never touched by sprays.

In consequence the cowslips and 'milkmaid', or cuckoo flowers, grow in abundance, buttercups too, and all the wild minty plants which flourished in every midland meadow before the advent of the farmers' sprays. This water meadow is grazed by cattle and sheep. The owner told me the flavour of the meat is quite different from that which comes from sprayed pastures. The cowslip has almost disappeared from the Midlands, it has gone with the buttercups and poppies.

I do not suppose I shall ever walk the 'quiet fields' in summer and find my shoes golden with pollen from the buttercups. Yet it was the buttercup roots which gave that unique flavour to mutton, a flavour which is often found now in Welsh mutton. I have watched Welsh sheep searching for the buttercup roots, disdaining the sweet mountain grass. I have an idea cattle avoided them, it was only sheep (and the woodpigeons) which ate them.

March 21 ————————————————————————

A Mr McMillan, a kind reader of my books, sent me recently two tails from the American ruffed grouse. These attractive game birds haunt the woodlands of Maine and elsewhere in USA and are famous for the drumming sound they make in the breeding season.

These tails, which I have now fixed to a wall of my study are spread like fans. The beauty of the pencilling and colouring is exquisite. I can only liken it to the sectrion of a mature tree trunk. On the outer edge there is a dark band three-quarters of an inch wide and below that are rings of rich brown becoming smaller towards the centre base, just as the growth rings on a tree butt show the age of the timber. It is as if the plumage copied the colours and lines of the severed oak trunk.

In the same way the owls and woodcock copy in their plumage the russets, greys and browns of the dead oak leaves and the November bracken hues. The artistry of nature always amazes me, how in most cases the colours harmonise and are 'in tune' as if the Great Designer of these things knew what was artistic and in harmony.

The same can be noticed in the plumage of other birds — contrast and harmony, features in which modern art seem singularly devoid. What better contrast could one find than the greys, blacks and whites of the grey plover, the simple contrast of black, blue, purple and white in the magpie, the exquisite tints in the cock wigeon? In bullfinches also, the soft blush of the pink breast contrasts with the grey back and black tail, and what dramatic contrasts there are in the wings of the red admiral butterfly — that brilliant orange red on the back wings and those spots of purest white!

I remember as a child looking at a blue-tit and marvelling at the lovely contrasts of blue, white, yellow and green. It reminded me of a butterfly and seemed infinitely desirable. I had a strange feeling I wanted to hold it in my hand, to fix that beauty in some way and keep it forever. It would be a difficult problem if one was asked which is the most beautiful British bird.

I would not give the verdict to the kingfisher, magnificent as it is. I would, I think, select the cock chaffinch in full spring plumage, partly because of the sense of 'restraint' in the colouring, nothing vulgar or obvious, and because that pure white on the shoulders adds exactly the finishing touch.

Many might be surprised at this selection and would say that the goldfinch was more attractive. But to my eyes the plumage of the goldfinch is perhaps a little overdone and complicated. The cock bullfinch and crossbill are lovely birds and some of the ducks are in the running but no, I plump for the cock chaffinch, he has my vote!

March 22 ─────────────────────────────

After days of bitter wind and putty-coloured sky, daughter Angela and I explored the Welland Valley in welcome sunlight.

At the little village of Welham we stopped by the old stone bridge to have our tea. The fields were green, distant plovers wheeled and dived, and in the distance sounded the continuous spring caw of rooks whose nests clothed the elm tops beyond the old church tower, and the thin plaint of lambs. I leant on the parapet of the bridge and looked down at the brown, sliding water big with flood.

A little way above the bridge the stream (for it is no more than a good-sized stream at Welham) took a bend to the left under willows and thorns. It reminded me of the infant Nene of my boyhood days which flowed in the valley below our house and which, incidentally, was the original 'Folly Brook' of my book the *Little Grey Men* which won the Carnegie Medal.

I thought back to those expeditions we made on summer days up the Nene, whose waters, like all Midland streams, are rarely clear but muddy ochre in colour.

What a truly magical thing was that stream! The very fact that you could not see down into the water as you can in west-country streams made it all the more exciting for fishing. The little quill float would coast gently down, revolving in the little bays, and suddenly dive from sight.

In nine cases out of ten it was a stickleback, sometimes a cluster, hanging to the brandling worm, but now and then you were rewarded by the real and longed-for prize, a bright and shining dace, as pristine as a new-minted sixpence piece. Occasionally, too, one would see a bullhead, an ugly spotted unfishlike creature with a toad-like head and barbules, with spines on its spotted back which could inflict a nasty jab to the grabbing triumphant hand. It was those dace which were the gems of the turgid little stream, one wondered how so bright and silver a fish could dwell in those muddy depths where the lumbering cattle sucked with their square mouths or stood belly-deep in the heat of midsummer to avoid the gadflies.

We built a dam of turves I remember, and it was there I learnt to swim. How triumphant I was one day when I found I could really swim without my knees on the muddy bottom! The pool was long and deep, but one year a summer flood came and washed it away. To a country boy streams, pools and woods were favourites, more than the lanes and the open fields.

The infant mind wondered what made the water hurry ever onwards, where did this everlasting supply originate, where was it going? The floating stick thrown in became a boat on a perilous voyage. It rushed along at a great pace in the shallows, sometimes its end caught upon some projecting weed or stick, then would swing out and on until it reached the pools on the bends, where it scarcely moved. If the stream ran high in the winter floods it might travel miles, it might even reach the open sea half a hundred miles away to the east! Sleeping or moving water held us in its spell.

In the big pond below the house of my childhood was a stone seat among the rushes where eighteenth-century squires sat and angled, a favourite spot with me on a hot summer afternoon. Fishing for roach one day at this spot I hooked a bright and kicking roachling, but before I could draw it up there appeared from the depths a monstrous spotted and barred object with a shovel mouth and cruel eye.

In a flash the fish was seized crosswise, the beanpole rod was snapped, a splash, a mighty swirl, and the pike departed and left me gasping and trembling with excitement.

My childish flimsy tackle was no match for such leviathans.

April 1 _____

For the very first time this year of
1980 the air is balmy, the goat
willows are golden and full of bees,
and at last I can smell the spring! How
appropriate this is on the first of April!

Angela and I, walking along the field road where we saw
the mallards on the bright pond, found ourselves surrounded
by old mother sheep and their children. The latter were
skipping and running races, full of the joy of being alive.

One lamb lay apart from the others, its head tucked round
asleep. As we stood and watched, it stirred and woke. Then it
did a strange thing. It seemed seized with fear. It lifted its head
skywards, peering about it as if it was sightless. Then it ran
round and round in tight circles and peered again at the sky.
Finally it blundered into the nearby ditch.

Was it really blind, I wondered? All the other lambs were
playing so happily, running races over the sweet green grass.
This waif seemed utterly distraught. Later I asked my friend
Bob, who has many sheep, whether the lamb could have
indeed been blind. No, he did not think so. He told me that,
like a sleeping child wakes suddenly and does not know where
it is, lambs will sometimes panic in this way, staring at the
sky and running in circles. Yet it did not bleat or call for
its mother.

When we returned later along the lane (noting the little
white violets just beginning to show in the southern facing
hedge bank) the little lamb was still there, gazing skywards in
all directions.

I have collected from Bob's garden pool a jar of frog-
spawn which I have put into my ponds. I expect the fish will eat
the tadpoles but some may survive. I have yet to see and hear

the toad I brought from Norfolk last autumn. It must be about somewhere under the ferns.

The quiet fields are now really green, the hedges showing the first signs of minute pale points, and the peewits call over the ploughlands.

April 3

The first swallow! A record for my nature diary. It flew over my car on this bright spring morning and, to set a seal to spring, the first brimstone appeared, which came to see me in my garden of all places! Later we saw others by the side of Bullocks Wood. What a joy to see once more those primrose-coloured wings which match exactly the first primrose showing in the woods. You will not see the brimstone in those dreary coniferous woods which each year seem to be multiplying because of the 'quick return' in cash. It is a true lover of the hard woods, the oak, beech, and ash. Oaks especially are often ivy grown, the favourite site for 'seeing the winter through', and these hibernated specimens are usually in perfect conditions.

The female is much paler, almost white, faintly tinged with yellow. A collector I knew once caught a brimstone whose wings were marked with orange.

This recurring miracle of spring is somehow so reassuring.

In many parts of the world where there is no spring, summer, autumn, or winter, as we understand it, what dull places they must be!

The hedges now are showing myriads of green leaves, each day the green new sword blades of the wild iris show more prominently and the fish are moving in Big Pond.

One resident moorhen continues to come for breakfast and calls to me each morning as I lie in bed 'Pruick!' and I answer it. Yet some days it is absent and will not stay to nest unless it can find a mate.

So far no frog croaks in the pond as it did last year, but

there is time enough, I see by my diary I did not hear a frog in Big Pond until April 15.

Two amusing things have happened over the filming of my book *Brendon Chase* now on location in the New Forest. A bear comes in the story of the three runaway boys. The producer tells me he interviewed the bear which came from Coventry and it sat in his chair!

Now I hear from friends who have just returned from camping in the New Forest that a farmer told them of a man who came to ask for a tow as his van was stuck in the Forest. He got the tow, by tractor, and when the van door was opened a bear appeared! My bear without a doubt, on location! I look forward to going down to the New Forest next month to watch the filming so I may meet the bear.

There is no sign of the frogs' spawn I put in my ponds, perhaps the moorhen knows something about it.

My purple emperor larvae which have been hibernating in their muslin cage in the garden have now left their 'seats' on the sallow stem and are going up to the growing sallow buds. They match these buds exactly both in shape and colour and are exceedingly difficult to see.

Six have never awakened, somehow they have become desiccated and, like the Cheshire cat in Alice in Wonderland, have faded away save for the two little horns. But I can count twelve on the tree with a possible thirteenth, which chose to hibernate in a dead leaf which I had to secure to the twig. This larva looks green so it may join its brethren on the buds, but it is a late starter.

I heard today of a wood in Wiltshire which the farmer owner decided to fell. A visiting naturalist found the rare black hairstreak there and before the trees were felled he managed to collect a large batch of eggs which were transferred to another wood.

Every year the habitats of our rarer insects and birds are done away with, and we have but a meagre number of British butterflies. Like the frogs they are vanishing, not only in Britain but in the USA and Canada. Nobody can throw any light on the disappearance of the frogs even in those countries where there is no agricultural spraying.

The black hairstreak is deemed to be considerably more rare than the purple emperor but is a butterfly very easily overlooked, being small and colourless, a drab little thing. Yet it frequents the same habitat as the purple emperor, as does the purple hairstreak which also loves sitting high in the forest oaks. The black hairstreak delights in the flowers of the wild privet. I once saw a bush covered with them in a large Midland forest. Our only true green butterfly is the green hairstreak, a delightful little fly. It is somewhat strange that there are so few green butterflies (and birds too for that matter) in Britain. I can only think of two green British birds, the green woodpecker and greenfinch, though the siskin has a little green in its plumage, as does the hen crossbill, and the greenshank is not really green.

April 14

Suddenly, in the middle of April, summer! Temperatures over 70°! The smell of summer already in the garden, the balsam poplar, its glistening sticky buds bursting, wafting its honey scent before the warm south wind, that same wind on which the swallows will be riding on their journey from Africa!

By every woodside the yellow flicker of brimstone wings, the bees busy in the golden tufted buds of the goat willows and lo! and behold! as I lay in bed last night with the window open wide, I heard 'coax! coax!' from Big Pond.

The frog was back, assuredly the frog that came last year on this very date, April 15! They must keep accurate watches in their waistcoat pockets to be so punctual for it is a fact that they will re-appear in spring on the exact date with the regularity of migrating birds.

All night long he sang earnestly from the pond, a voice I have not heard for so long and which was so familiar in my boyhood days, a voice as friendly as that of a cricket on the hearth.

I went to the window and looked out on the sleeping garden on this warm spring night.

The stars burned dimly over the big willow, the water gleamed dully in the shadows, the balsam poplar perfume dominated all.

'Coax! coax!' came from the periwinkle jungle that lines the pond, wooing a mate maybe, calling for one! There was something about that cheerful rustic voice in the night which gave me great pleasure, a sound which was so familiar in that lovely vanished world before man ruined the countryside with his sprays of poison. That frog felt good to be about in the fragrant darkness among the mints and weeds by the pondside as he hearkened to the drums of spring and voiced his satisfaction and desires. And a little later my unbelieving ear caught an answering echo, another frog was calling from the smaller garden pond on the lawn, so I have two pilgrims of the spring to serenade me!

I remember how last autumn I brought a toad from Norfolk and released it by Big Pond. I wondered if it had found a mate. Certainly the vocalists in the pond were not toads, for the latter has no voice cords but is nevertheless capable of making a small noise especially when frightened.

From my window I could see on the lawn the dim white stars of the weeping cherry like arrested snowflakes, and beyond that the sleeping quiet fields, beyond that again the dark loom of the forest.

Rings widened and gleamed on the surface of the Big Pond where no doubt the big carp was exploring the marginal weeds, busy on his nocturnal explorations. No breeze moved the trees.

As I stood in the window the village clock struck two to remind me of the inexorable passage of the hours. Earlier, with daughter Angela, I had explored a new wood, one I had only seen from afar but which looked interesting.

The afternoon was as warm as June, but surprisingly few birds were singing. I do not think I have ever been in such a dense and tangled wood, it was an example of what can happen to woodland if it is neglected, and the underbrush left to run riot.

The rides were marked with the neat spoor of fallow deer, but there was little bird life visible or audible, only wood-pigeons which clattered away through the ash poles. These birds had evidently been having a midday siesta and we had stirred them up.

It must have been to the advantage of a pigeon shooter whom we later saw ensconced in a hide under a clump of elms with twelve decoys spread out on the dry orange plough. For at intervals came shots, doubles and singles, so we were doing him a good turn and the pigeons an ill one.

In some parts of this tangled wood were clearings in which stood massive oak trees, but in the main the trees were hidden by thickets of blackthorn which, because of the dense canopy overhead, had died from lack of light and so formed an impenetrable thorny barrier through which even the stoutest dog could not force a passage, and nothing larger than a weasel or a mouse could go. The only traveller we met in this shadow-banded ride was a plodding brimstone butterfly, glad to be out in the sunlight after its long sojourn in some ivy-clad oak.

Here and there the sallows were in full bloom, loud with bees, showing golden against the tangle of bare oak twigs, ashes, and the thickets of blackthorn. Much of the latter was in bud, some full out, as white as snow.

Usually cold winds blow at the blackthorn flowering, not so this spring, we have had no 'blackthorn winter'.

Yet this snatch of summer must be short lived, soon we shall be back again in the cold east winds which sometimes blow until May is out. I will not be deceived. So we must make the most of this shining hour. In the village allotments red-faced men are working in their shirt sleeves, turning the dried soil, real countrymen who love the country, some ploughing with the new-fangled motor ploughs, other digging deep with shining spades, spades which have been cleaned and cherished, even oiled, during the useless days of winter.

There will be a goodly harvest in mid-June worth temp-orary back-aches, ivory-coloured potatoes the size of hens' and

pigeons' eggs with a flavour never to be found in those we buy from shops, a flavour so delicate and delicious one can go on eating them forever. There will be beans later, following the scarlet flowers which climb the sticks and sweet lettuce, snappy and juicy, and tender spring onions like fairies' dumb bells, valiant accompaniments to good ale and cheese after the day's end.

April 19

My frog has become less vocal, though he had a companion, judging from the answering croaks from the moist thickets at the top of Big Pond. Strange to say I have seen no swallows since the single one which flew over my car on April 3.

My purple emperor larvae are now up on the opening buds and feeding well and have already lost the 'brown bark' camouflage of hibernation. As far as I can see, I have a dozen healthy larvae. I lost at least seven or eight when they failed to awaken in the early spring. I can only think I made a mistake in covering the top of the muslin cage to keep out the heavy rain and snow.

The camouflage of this rare insect is amazing from the time it hatches from the egg until emergence in July and August. At the present moment they closely resemble the half-opened leaves of the sallow which have painted tips, and as the larvae are the exact colour and shape of the sallow buds they are practically invisible. Even the chrysalises resemble a sallow leaf and are then more difficult to see than at any other time, unless it is when they are in hibernation, for then they resemble a fold of sallow bark.

I have recently bought a Weeping Salix (*Caprea pendula*). As this is more compact it should fit well into a breeding cage. The normal sallow (*Caprea*) has to be severely pruned to prevent the branches touching the muslin walls of the cage, which is fatal as it provides a 'walk in' for vermin and a 'walk out' for larvae.

I had close on sixty eggs last season from my reserve, but only twelve have come through. Only recently I discovered the probable loss of larvae. On taking down the cage door to inspect my stock yesterday I noticed to my horror a series of large holes in the muslin at the top edge. No doubt earwigs and spiders entered through these apertures in the autumn and helped themselves. I have now stuck a strip of muslin over the holes with a waterproof gum but it is like closing the stable door when the horse has departed.

Now, near April's end, the hedges are dressed in new green, well forward I think compared to previous years. I have known few green hedges at the end of April in some years but the hot weather we enjoyed recently over Easter brought out the buds.

April 24 ─────────────────────────────────

When I was bending down to inspect a faulty beer tap in the cellar this morning I felt my 'back' go. I have had this trouble off and on for years, a certain small movement seems to rip a muscle somewhere near the spine.

Result! I am now in bed and practically immovable. There will be many readers who have experienced this dire complaint, of a 'bad back'. I was virtually pole-axed, even getting to bed called for great fortitude. So now here I am with a calm spring evening outside and the only thing to look at, the budding upper boughs of my laburnum in the garden.

We take good health very much for granted, it is only on these occasions when the body 'plays up' that we realize what it means to be totally deprived of motion, even vacating my bed is an ordeal and a cough or sneeze quite calamitous. The annoying thing is that I feel so well in myself. The frog still croaks in the pond and its cheerful voice makes it even harder to stay immobile like this, as helpless as an old sheep turned on its back.

The doctor arrived and gave me an injection which is supposed to deaden the pain, and multitudes of pills. So, hey ho! I must be patient and long for the day I can enjoy the quiet fields once more. How dependent we are on our bodies and their functioning!

I would not be surprised to see a swallow go past the window — in the meantime I must look at the laburnam crown where occasionally a house-sparrow perches on the twigs.

A forest walk yesterday was rewarded by a colony of cowslips growing in a sequestered corner, I have some by me as I write. Cowslips, like the frogs, are becoming rarer each year — their fragrance is a true scent of spring. They only grow now in those places where no agricultural sprays can get at them.

There was an ancient parish boundary mound near here which was thick with the fragrant yellow bells every spring. Now this has been ploughed up. I know no other place near home where they can be found, save in that forest lawn. This long green mound had been there since all the land about here was part of the great forest of Rockingham in medieval times. Close by, one can still see the traces of what was once the forest ranger's lodge wherein dwelt the King's forest keeper in the fourteenth century. One can still trace the foundations, and the dried-up hollow which was once a fishpond is still clearly visible. For miles around my present house was once part of the great forest of Rockingham. There is a record of the parson of those days who was had up for poaching the Kings' deer. He was caught red-handed with a bow and dead fallow buck. The records do not state what happened to this unlucky cleric — no doubt because of his calling he was 'put on probation'.

Poaching the deer still goes on today. My old friend Tub, the local keeper, tells me he found some deer snares only the other week, set in a dense part of the forest. The snares of wire are set in the secret runways of the deep thickets. The poor deer must suffer greatly if they get their heads in the noose for they die by slow strangulation. In one part of the woods there is a high deer fence around some experimental tree plantings. In the wire mesh some friends found a fallow buck caught by its horns in this high barricade — it has to be high to prevent the deer jumping over.

I do not know why we get no roe in these woods. There are plenty of the little hump-backed Japanese deer which I often see in the late evenings up the dark ridings, those mysterious gloomy corridors where the close crowding firs give a midnight darkness on even the brightest summer day.

These gnome-like tusked deer have little of the grace of the fallow deer, for their backs are humped, giving them a deformed appearance. They are little bigger than a large hare and, like hares, extremely good to eat. Though their bodies are misshapen, their legs are as slender and exquisitely fashioned as those of all the deer family.

In the summer of 1979, daughter Angela and I paid a visit to Phil Drabble at his home in the Staffordshire woodlands where he has five hundred acres surrounded by a ring fence. The fallow deer come to be fed in winter, the muntjac deer as well. Drabble had a baby muntjac which was very tame and trotted up to us to have his head scratched.

That lovely June day he took us all round the boundaries of his ground; no naturalist could visualize a more delectable home as this on the Bagot estate. Not only has he the wild deer as friends but soon after he bought his house, some herons arrived and founded a colony in one of his woods.

From the large picture window of the house we looked across to an oak-fringed lake and quiet green rides giving delightful vistas between the oaks of feeding deer — one a white one. Ducks and Canada geese swam on the lake. Phil told me the deer came up to the table in front of the picture window in winter to feed.

Some of the oaks on his land must be of great age, some are stag headed, always the sign of age, which in an oak can be over half a thousand years. Details of his lovely house can be found in his book *No Badgers In My Wood* published by Michael Joseph in 1979 to which I wrote a foreword.

April 27

After twelve months of bachelordom our moorhen cock appeared this morning with a girlfriend in tow! There was great excitement all day. He married her at least six times and they swam about Big Pond with white tails fanning. Some of the time he sat on the nest while she swam about. There were frequent pursuits around the apple trees with the hen assuming the mating posture, head down, back arched.

The cock seemed absurdly happy and contented. When he was not pursuing the girlfriend he sat on the lawn and preened, but if she went off he hastened to find her, flirting his tail and calling. For the last three weeks he has been very restless, calling frequently and being absent for half a day or more. So now he has at last found a mate I am hoping all will go well. He has already laid the foundations of a nest in the middle of the wild iris clump where the previous birds had several broods.

The jab the doctor gave me two days ago, together with nearly five pounds' worth of pills, seem to be curing the back trouble, and I can walk without a stick. I was able to walk round the garden and sniff the soft spring scents of bursting buds and balsam leaves which fill the whole garden with their heavy scent of honeycomb.

This rush of fresh spring smells after the scentless days of winter is part of my enjoyment on this threshold of summer.

April 28

The course of true love rarely runs smoothly.

The moorhen's girlfriend does not seem to take kindly to Big Pond. He sits on a half-made empty nest whilst she wanders aimlessly about the garden, disappearing at intervals into the hedge. When this occurs he leaves his brooding and goes to find her, calling all the time. I fear she will lure him across the road with fatal results.

At one time this morning they sat side by side as he tickled her neck. He is obviously in love, but desires more than anything to start a family. Last night after she left him he sulked and went to roost up the birch tree by the pond. Where she went I know not, but she returned after dawn. Now she has gone again.

Because of the long toes on the moorhens' foot, they have to walk like a mannequin is supposed to do, putting one foot carefully in front of the other. If they walked like we do, their long claws would catch each other. The same applies to coot and heron, and to a lesser extent to the ducks. That is why the duck has a waddling gait, rolling from side to side in a nautical manner.

The courtship of some birds seems to be quite a lengthy process, as it is with the human race, though not with pheasants! The 'Chase me Charlie' method of the hen moorfowl continues for several days. Once mated they are devoted to each other — I believe for life.

Certainly my visiting male bird, which has been with us off and on all winter, had no mate then. His present girlfriend has by no means said yes. We shall see. I look upon this little romance with interest. It certainly helps to lighten these dreary cold days when from morning to night the sun is veiled by cloud and there is a chill wind, the 'blackthorn winter' wind at last, blowing from the east.

Yet, despite the lack of sun, the blossoms are as snow on my pear and cherry trees and the new red chestnut purchased in the winter shows signs of flower buds.

April 29 _____

What can I say of this fearful grey winter weather with its mizzling rain borne on a cruel east wind? It seems to make a mockery of the thick green hedgerows, now fully out, and the flowering wild crabs and cherries. It seems that such days, which should be so precious to anyone over middle age, are wasted ones.

One cannot enjoy the open air, there is little to see, even the birds seem absent from the gardens — it is truly winter in the middle of late spring. Even those subtle scents of growing things are absent.

My moorhen pair have disappeared (though they were on Big Pond first thing) and I have nothing to watch but a single fat ring-dove, which has been gorging on the ivy berries on the old apple tree at the top of the garden, clumsily flapping about among the thick shiny leaves. This again was quite a winter scene. There you are — the blackthorn is still in full bloom, and until it rusts winter will still be with us. There are no swallows — not since the solitary one I saw on April 3.

Angela swears she heard the cuckoo last evening — late — calling from the forest. I doubt it and suspect a collared dove.

She brought me yesterday a jar full of toad tadpoles given to us by a friend — the postmaster at Thrapston. I have put these in one of the smaller ponds and hope they will survive and multiply though toads do not croak like the frogs — there is still one 'coaxing' in the middle pond, but his performance must be nearly over — once April is out he will fall silent.

To help pass these dreary house-bound hours I have been reading Kilvert's *Diary* again, whose descriptions of the countryside and atmosphere of the seasons match the writing of any other author — even of Hudson and Jefferies.

One entry which somehow held me is that for New Year's Eve, 1871, when Kilvert, his brother Perch and his mother, stood at the door of Langley Burrel Rectory listening to the bells of Chippenham which came 'faintly and muffled over the snow'. 'It was bitter cold but we went to the door, Perch and I, to hear better. I was carrying my travelling clock in my hand and so we stood on the terrace just outside the front door, the little clock struck midnight. We thought we could hear three peals of church bells, Chippenham, St Paul's, and very faintly, Kington. "Ring happy bells across the snow".'

What magic power there is in writing like this which can

conjure up so exactly — over the arch of years, the thin tinkling ping, ping, sound of Kilvert's 'travelling clock' and the distant bells in the snowy night!

My father, who was also a parson, was ten years old on that night, with a life before him of over eighty years and of changes in the world beyond the wildest imaginings. Nature-wise, it has become a far inferior place due to the folly and greed of mankind, where, even though through marvellous reasoning we have put men on the moon and brought them back, we are as far away as ever from solving how to regulate our lives and live in peace with our fellow men.

Another entry from Kilvert's *Diary* dated May 24, 1875, caught my eye. 'As I came down from the hill into the valley across the golden meadows and along the flower-scented hedges a great wave of emotion and happiness stirred and rose up within me. I know not why I was so happy, nor what I was expecting but I was in a delirium of joy, it was one of the supreme moments of existence, a deep delicious draught from the strong sweet cup of life.

'It came unsought, unbidden, at the meadow stile, it was one of the flowers of happiness scattered for us and found unexpectedly by the wayside of life. It came silently and suddenly and it went as it came but left a long lingering glow of glory behind it as it faded slowly ... and I shall ever remember the place and the time in which such great happiness fell upon me.'

I was interested in this entry, for I well remember three or four occasions in my early life when I experienced these exact sensations — sensations which were never repeated after middle age. I can find no explanation for this — others may have had the same experience. Why, at this time of the year, at the very threshold of green summer, I should have been so taken with these entries I do not know — I must blame it on this 'little winter', I suppose.

The skies clearing a little, I walked up to the forest — now sadly scarred and marred by the visiting horse people who poach up the ridings so that it is difficult for foot people, and a sprained ankle threatens the walker. Absolute silence there — not a bird singing or moving but the sallows a fresh green, and the primroses out, showing yellow splashes amongst last November's leaves. The only bird song I heard was a mistle-thrush singing in the firs in my garden — a suitable enough song for such harsh and unkind weather, for they seem to like the challenge of the east wind. They are the first to sing in winter and will do so when song-thrush and blackbird remain silent.

What a fine bold bird it is, so much bigger than the gentle song-thrush, his very posture on the bough is defiant — striped breast thrust out like a boxer's and head held high.

May 3 ──────────────

The moorhen's love story has taken a
new turn.

She came back to him on April 30
and they were happy and busy on the pond.
Then she vanished. Ever since, he has been looking
for her — not on the pond but always standing across the
lawn from it, in the herbaceous border. For three days he has
kept daily vigil but no sign of his true love. Perhaps some
dark fate has overtaken her, a cat, fox or motor car.

I doubt if he will stay with us much longer unless he finds
another wife or she comes back.

She was rather a flighty little thing — leaving the garden
for hours at a time. It is sad to see his misery — he stands
hunched up among the growing delphiniums and rarely visits
the pond ten yards distant, even water has no charms for
him. This again is puzzling, yet I feel the romance has not
ended yet.

The cruel east wind still blows, but there is more sun. I see
the blackthorn still flowers, so there is hope.

May 4 ──────────────────────

A brilliant morning but with a stiff east wind. A walk in Far
Forest — the rides fresh with new grass, shadows from newly
opened leaves dappling the forest paths down which three
fallow hinds went galloping, to the amazement of my labrador Polar.

In the shadows of the fresh green sallows there suddenly

fell upon the air like the strokes of a fairy bell the notes of a nightingale. It is some three years since I heard one in the forest — once there were at least half a dozen breeding pairs but now we only seem to get the birds on passage. A willow warbler was singing too among the sallows. When we got home our swallow was sitting on the telephone wire, so the glass in the garage door was hastily removed so they can fly in and out. I have yet to hear the cuckoo, though others in the village have heard it and David Nash, the Duke's keeper, told me he had heard it in Grafton Wood last week.

In Far Forest this morning the sun was hot, one would never have guessed a chill east wind blew outside. Hardly a leaf moved in the dappled ridings. There was a fragrance of growing things, grass leaves and blossom on the wild crabs.

To our amazement the erring moorhen wife returned today — she was on the pond first thing and the pair were happily reunited all day. Now she has vanished again and he is back on the herbaceous border on the look-out for her, appearing disconsolate and lonely.

May 12

The frog serenades me all through these hot May nights. I love to hear him as I lie in bed. We are plunged into summer — the sun shines all day and a brisk hot wind from the south bends and bows my poplar spires until at evening it dies away and the cuckoo calls from the forest across the quiet fields. I delight in the voice of this frog, it pleases me as much as a bird's song, and another answers it from Big Pond.

I lie awake with the window wide open, feeling the soft night air on my face. The stars shine beyond the dark, tassled crowns of the Scotch firs and that cheerful voice continues unwearying. I do not know what powers of hearing the frog possesses but it seems to me they call against each other. From time to time they fall silent and then I picture them catching insects and other creatures among the damp mints and weeds of the pond-side and sleeping garden.

As to the moorhen romance, it is still on and off. She appears each day and is chased around — sometimes they stand flank to flank and tickle each other's napes — nibbling gently like cart-horses tickle each other's necks. But she does not seem to stay any length of time, but is off again to leave him to his vigil in the herbaceous border. I am delighted to say that two swallows are investigating my studio with the idea of setting up house. This is a little difficult, for our deep freeze is in there and the door will have to be kept open if they decide to build.

I was disgusted and cross the other day to read of a woman who was writing in a woman's paper to ask advice as to how to keep house-martins from building under the eaves of her house. I would give a good deal to have these little white rumpled people seeking hospitality under my roof. I even put up imitation house-martins nests to encourage them but only the house-sparrows came — no martins.

In a neighbouring parish, swallows built year after year in the church porch. When I visited the church the other day I was disgusted to see the rafters and ledges had been wired in to prevent the birds entering. I hope the parson will be up for judgement after his departure from this lovely world for he has banished birds which must have been familiar to the founder of the Christian faith. It is a bird which I regard as sacred, and a regular visitor to the Holy Land. A box or tray could easily be fastened under the next to catch the droppings and the stone flags wiped clean in a moment.

It reminded me of another person — a woman with a hen-pecked husband. He was delighted when house-martins arrived at their new house and built a nest under the eaves but the wife took a broom and knocked the nest down for fear the 'patio' would be soiled by the droppings.

A few yards from my garden's end, across the road, is a small brook from which originally my moorhens came. At one

angle of it there is a miniature beach — a fairy shore of sand and mud, free from the fragrant wild thyme leaves which grow abundantly there.

Here I watch the swallows and martins gather in these hot days of early summer. They alight daintily, holding up their tails as though they were skirts, for their legs are short and they must not sully their white underpants. They skilfully gather their little plastic pellets. When they have enough they take wing over the waving corn bound for their nesting sites.

It is such a summer scene, with the shuttling shadows from the overhanging hawthorns and the giant ash tree whose leaves are just beginning to break (like the walnut it is a cautious tree afraid of late frosts). The water sparkles with many brilliant stars as it talks its way among the thick-growing moisture-loving herbage, brook lime, and water mints.

In the hot noonday there is great activity among these blue-backed travellers who only a few short weeks ago were hawking over African lagoons. Their lives must be advent-urous and enjoyable, so unlike the garden robins and black-birds who are pedestrians by comparison, as I am.

Those little brilliant eyes have seen so much — far more than I shall ever see — elephants, egrets, buffalo and lion, zebra, and giraffe. They have felt the merciless power of the African sun and witnessed many a spectacular sunset over mountain and desert. Truly an exciting, if brief, life so dif-ferent to my own. Can you wonder I delight to see them and feel privileged to offer them hospitality in my garage and sheds?

May 16 ────────────────────────────────

Hopes are rising over my studio swallows! I see a half-moon of mud pellets are being cemented high up near the ceiling below a nail. There is much to-ing and fro-ing these peerless sunny mornings (we are enjoying days of unprecedented unbroken sunshine), and last night a cautious peep showed bird and wife roosting — one on the 'nest' nail, the other on another handy nail close by.

This is the first time they have ever chosen my studio for nesting. It means I dare not work there for fear of disturbing them, and our visits to the deep freeze must be few and far between.

It means, also, if I am painting, that I shall have to work in the house. No matter! This I am glad to do for the privilege of having this lovely wedded pair deigning to ask for hospitality under my roof. What puzzles me is how they first got their plasterwork to stick to the smooth vertical wall for the mud 'half ring' so far completed is below the large nail above, so they could not have perched on this. Their small feet could find no purchase on the smooth wall. Whether the nail will be incorporated into the finished house I do not know; it is not as if the wall was of brick or stone.

As to the moorhen saga — there are still no definite signs of serious house-keeping, though the old man is always about and the flighty wife comes and goes as she pleases.

A gamekeeper friend rang me last night in great excitement to say that an osprey has been catching fish in the lake near his house not ten miles distant from my house — no doubt on passage. He told me he had just seen the osprey pass his house carrying a large bream. It flew with it into some firs near the lake.

If it continues to haunt the place I will be over. It is one of our rarities I have never seen. I do not broadcast the fact for fear of armies of bird-watchers descending on the estate, which would not please the owners nor the keeper. The swifts have come, I saw the first a week ago.

The intense activity on these summer mornings in my garden is a constant delight. The moorhens active on the pond, frogs croaking in the pools, young blackbirds being fed — collared doves ferrying sticks to a nest in the old ivy-clad apple tree, song-thrushes nesting in the firs, and my blue-backed swallows sweeping into my garage with their pellets of mud.

There is a wonderful sense of upsurging life — the trees bursting into full leaf — the apple blossom a glory of pink and white, and even two strong spikes of red chestnut blossom on the newly planted tree outside the french windows. What joy — what promise there is in this glorious spring! The only sad note is that I have not heard the cuckoo again and know it has been poisoned by the farmers' sprays.

My peach tree on the west wall is covered with set fruit — the long hot spell has suited it well and it gives promise of a great fruit harvest at summer's end. This is mainly due to the expert pruning of my good friend Len Shipley who attended to it last November when I was away goose-hunting in the north, and my diligent spraying against leaf curl last October and again in February. Also, when on a walk the other day down a country road, I discovered many horse droppings on the marginal grass and a convenient plastic bag near-by was quickly filled. The manure is now round the base of my peach — which incidentally is a 'Peregrine' and produces huge luscious peaches as large as tangerines.

The purple emperor larvae in my net cage are now in their third instar — this I think is due to the hot weather. It seems only a day or so ago that they were minute, hardly visible, grubs, their colour matching the drab winter bark of the sallow. Now they are nearly an inch long, exactly the colour of the new sallow leaves, with slanting yellow stripes on their sides, quite handsome creatures regally formed, like fairy bulls.

May 18

This amazing summer continues with scarcely a cloud.

Last night I looked in at my studio at my swallow pair. One was roosting on a nail near the nest — the other — probably the female on the rim, both asleep. They go to bed early, as well they might, for they have had a long and tiring day visiting the 'cement works' and all the labour of building.

Whilst late blackbirds are still warbling in the dusky garden, the swallow pair have long gone to roost. Before they sleep they burble and chatter together, no doubt discussing the doings of the day. What dreams take place in those delicate craniums? I am sure birds dream as do dogs and men.

Maybe they dream of arid desert wastes and perilous journeys over snow-clad alps, of treacherous heavy seas, of pyramids, and palm trees dark against a red sunset. But they will be awake long before me, for there is still much house-building to complete — the nest must be lined with feathers gathered from the farmyards in the village and perhaps scraps of sheep's wool from the wayside hedge.

Still my frogs croak all through these hot nights — a sound which might be confused with the yapping of distant terriers and toy dogs.

Now, along the waysides that border the quiet fields the dandelions are going to seed. A week ago the roadside margins were golden with them, now the petals have fallen and they have gone to seed. I pluck these seed heads for my pet bullfinches who delight in them, they are as delicious to them as asparagus is to us.

If one looks closely at these seed clumps you will notice that seventy per cent have been already eaten by birds and mice, the base of the flower mere hollow shells.

Goldfinches and greenfinches, as well as bullfinches and sparrows, are great dandelion-seed eaters. They skilfully detach the seed from the ends of the silky white filaments — the latter, discarded threads of silvery silk-like 'parachutes', also make good nest linings. The mice come at night and run nimbly up the stalks — they too delight in the tiny pointed seeds.

I remember before the Second World War, seeing acres of golden dandelions lining the banks of the Dutch polders near the famous bridge of Arnhem, scene of desperate battles during the last days of the War. Many variegated ruffs were displaying among the golden flowers, apparently ignored by their women folk.

This week and next is surely the cream of the year. Every wayside country road is fringed with a forest of white chervil or ladies' bedstraw. Usually about this time the local council people cut down these fragrant weeds, but possibly from economy reasons the margins remain uncut this summer.

The laburnum and the white and red may is in full splendour, the chestnuts are alight from top to bottom with cream and red cones of blossom. In the cool green shade I watch the cattle stand and lie, for they distrust the sunlit field and its stinging flies.

I lay awake this morning at four a.m. It was already light — the garden cloaked in a mysterious greyness, silent save for a lusty cuckoo which was perched among the apple blossom of my old trees. Cuckoos — like the human inhabitants of Norway and Sweden — make the most of the light and sometimes sing all night like the sedge warbler and nightingale. Whilst he sang again and again that evocative double note, I knew that in my studio, high up on the dim wall, my little swallow pair were still a-bed watching through sleepy eyes the grey light through the open window.

The cuckoo, lazy sponger of the bird world (which has its counterpart in the human race), has no work to do — no nest to build or young to feed and rear, for him it is a glorious social security set-up. He has nothing to do but enjoy himself and let others do the work.

It is true the female has the task of nest hunting, but that entails no hard labour. She simply sits on a bush or willow and keeps her eyes and ears open for a victim, and the egg is soon laid. Wherever one walks in the woods, lanes, and quiet fields you can smell the scent of hawthorn and wild cherries — it is what I call the hawthorn wind. Mingled with it is the scent of wild apple blossom and rape, for all around, the Midland fields are ablaze with the harsh crude yellow of the rape flowers whose smell is vaguely unpleasant to some, just as is the smell of elder flowers. I do not object to it — it is a summer smell, reminiscent perhaps of untarred leather or perspiring horses.

The white petals of the hawthorn fall to the dark water of my Big Pond, forming rafts which drift before the summer breezes. They fall into the brook across the road to voyage on to join the Nene and (perhaps) ultimately the sea. This is the time when the wayside and meadow grasses are soft, erect, and of a beautiful rich green — the new minted green which so soon fades and darkens.

I have often wished it would be possible in paint to give the essence of this lush and complicated growth — Dürer tried to do so in a water colour of great beauty. It is in the shade of trees that the soft green is most luxuriant and delicious — the millions of erect aromatic grasses like the pile of an even-turfed carpet contrasting with the sunlit fields beyond which, in some southern counties, there is still a fine glow of buttercups.

Standing in the cool shade where flies lazily jig together, the sunlight gilds the edges of the splayed leaves of the horse-chestnuts. Look up under the rich canopy above, and all manner and shades of soft green can be seen with here and there the dark ropes of branches crossing and re-crossing. Little wonder the cattle and sheep like to seek out this cool parlour rather than face the blinding glare of the sunlit pasture.

The cuckoo's voice comes with monotonous regularity. I have counted overy fifty 'cuckoos' in one burst of singing — like distant bells floating across the quiet summer fields.

Relish these days for they are more precious than you think; they should be savoured as the seconds pass like vintage wine. Tomorrow the skies may be grey and the winds cold, for such is our fickle climate and there will be no soft shadows under the chestnuts, or cattle, or a distant cuckoo bell over buttercup fields. In a fortnight's time it will be mid-summer and the longest day, and the sun will begin its inexorable journey away from us.

I visualize this quiet field, in the dreary winter days when it is dark at four in the afternoon! Then the great chestnuts will be black and glistening in the rain, each bare twig holding a silver drop — the sodden grass a muddy ochre, the cattle away in the yards.

So I stand awhile and drink in this glowing summer scene — surely there is no other country in this round ball of the world which holds such charm and magic and sense of summer's splendour?

May 31

The moorhen saga is not quite over.

I have noticed both birds secretly entering a shady hollow under a splayed beech bough on Little Pond, just opposite my window as I write. The cock has been seen carrying in nesting material, and the hen also. They have evidently come to regard the nest site on Big Pond as too exposed. Moorhens are most secretive birds and I hope that, after all, they have a nest there. We shall see. As the pond is not more than a couple of feet from the window I can observe these goings-on unseen.

The vociferous frogs have at last ceased to croak. I miss their midnight friendly voices, so cheerful, musical and reassuring.

I rejoice also to hear the muted murmuring love talk of my wedded swallow pair in my studio. By day the male is away fly-catching, but each late evening he returns to his brooding mate perched on a nail close by the nest, and there he talks to her until they fall asleep. It is a sweet song, a true lullaby. Mrs Swallow listens attentively — her little round head facing him over the edge of the nest.

I fully realize that I shall be barred from the studio until the young fly, and that in the future years left to me it is almost certain that they and their children will return. Here they are sure of a welcome and consideration, and I must alter my working arrangements to suit them.

In any case, I do not paint much in the summer months — it is more of a winter occupation. When those dreary sunless days return and my guests have gone following the sun they worship, I can look up from my easel and see that cunningly constructed mud house high up on the north wall and wonder where the owners are — Spain, Africa, or Egypt. May the Great Spirit watch over them.

June 8

The moorhen saga is reaching its climax. Whilst both birds were up on Big Pond I made a 'recce' among the moist thickets at the top end of Little Pond opposite our windows — not twelve feet distant.

A spray of beech overhangs there, forming a fan-like screen. Beneath this, cunningly hidden among the periwinkle, was a substantial nest as full to the brim with eggs as a hen wife's shopping basket! These cunning fowl had built it there — possibly in these early summer mornings when it is light at four a.m., for we have seen no nest building during the daylight hours. I had noticed a suspicious dark channel in the green duck weed leading under the spray.

So now all is made plain.

The flighty hen has been brought to bed and in the fullness of time, within a day or so, I expect to see the first little blackamoor emerge. All that chasing around the apple trees and about the lawn in those April days seems to be coming to fruition. I am delighted, for last summer we had no broods — only the mourning male.

He sometimes takes wing out of the garden and is absent for long periods but he takes his turn at incubating and there is a definite changing of the guard. Cats will get short shrift if I spy one in the garden, for they do come at times from the cat-infested village. Young moorhens are greatly fancied by cats.

The white ladies' bedstraw along the waysides have gone to seed — suddenly — during the last two days, but my walnut tree is still almost naked — the leaves only just beginning to expand. It is the latest of all the trees to come to full leaf — even later than the ash, for it is susceptible to the late frosts. The hedgerows also are losing their fresh-minted green and the woods are darkening to their midsummer hue. With so little rain and an abundance of sun the pastures are almost like those of July — the yellow rape flowers have gone but red may and laburnum are in their full glory.

As for the swallows in my studio, they are still brooding eggs, and each night the male continues to sing to his wife until dusk and drowziness overtakes him. The frogs have ceased to sing but the cuckoos — abundant this year — are still calling from the forest. So goes the summer on.

The hot windless weather is hopeless for the fly fishers. I went last week to the Eye Brook Reservoir. The water was a polished mirror full of floating scabs of green algae. Not a fish was to be seen. We lazed in the boat, listening to dreamy cuckooing from the woods on the east bank.

Ony towards sun-setting did a fish seize my sunken fly. The rod point bowed to the water as the fish fought all round the boat, now below the stern, then to port and starboard. I never saw this fish so could not guess its size — only once seeing a sudden flash of gold far down in the green water.

After some eight minutes' battle the rod point flew up. The fish had gone — it had taken me right down to the backing and with the long stern struggle the hook must have pulled free. A moment later my fishing fly buried itself in my little finger and I spent a gory interval tearing it free. It was a small hook so I could not push it right through a fold of my skin to cut the barb which is the best way of dealing with accidents of this kind. Many people have been blinded by flying hooks imbedding themselves in the eye — this often occurs in a high wind so it is wise to wear glasses when fly fishing.

Still, hot days with cloudless skies are hopeless for trout fishing — a dull warm windy day is best — often with rain and a good 'sea' running.

I never like to see what a fishing friend of mine calls 'Kelly's Diamonds' — those small round clots of foam forming windrows. But the rougher the day the better — it seems to stir the trout up from the deeps. The wind blows flies down on to the surface of the water.

June 9 ————————————————————————————————

A sharp note from Little Pond just below my bedroom window suggested that dark deeds were afoot. The time was a little past three a.m. I had been roused from a deep sleep.

By standing on a chair it was possible to look down on the upper end of the pond. The summer night was already dim with the coming dawn. I could see no disturbance on the pond but the alarm note — an urgent 'quik quik' repeated at intervals — continued.

Next morning I saw both birds on the lawn and, as I watched, the male came slowly back to Little Pond. He swam up to the nest entrance under the beech spray — peered in and swam away again.

Later, I examined the nest. It was no longer full of eggs — the nest was disturbed. Only three cold eggs remained. Some rat, cat, or other vermin had evidently raided the nest — the most likely villain would be a rat.

The mourning pair hung about the lawn all day and at the end of the afternoon both departed over the firs to the nearby stream. So it looks as if all my high hopes of watching the family hatch and grow have been dashed.

I have bushed in the big iris clump on Big Pond with branches of fir to give privacy which they had hitherto lacked. They have a 'rest' nest there built by the cock in the spring, and my only hope is that they will chance a second brood in this new site where two years ago the cock — happily married then with a steady wife — reared two broods in the summer of 1978. We shall see. I have a feeling that the story of my moorhens is not quite over.

At least my swallow family in the studio are well and active, and that is some compensation.

How absurd it would seem to the great majority of people

that I should feel such a sense of loss over the ravaged moorhens' nest, but I was so looking forward to seeing the little black balls emerge, waving their little flippers to their parents. The truth is this new wife is a flighty nervous little thing — so different to his old mate who was killed on the road. It is her fault entirely that they did not choose the iris clump on Big Pond where the other pair successfully reared two broods in 1978, when he wanted to nest.

These tragedies of the wild are echoed equally with ourselves, and myself in particular, having lost both my wife and small son through the vicious blows of chance. Some people sail through life without trouble, but they are the exception. Joy and sorrow are as natural as winter and summer. It is well to remember this and not rebel against it, all life is at risk from birth to death.

June 11

The first wild rose of summer! And a wonderful June it has been — what I call a 'childhood' June, when the sun shines with all its full glory, and distant trees and woods are muffled in a blue glaze — each tree surrounded by a sort of halo, the centre of the tree being of a darker tone — a delightful thing to express in oil paint on canvas. This is most evident when the sun is overhead.

That shy pink rose in the tangle of the hedge told me more than anything how the summer is passing, so do the flat crumbly plates of the elder flowers, creamy in colour and with their wild insistent tangy scent, opening flat along the wayside bordering the quiet fields.

The wild roses of the north country and the Highlands — and the west country too — have a much richer, more vivid colour, not so attractive as the 'blushing' pink of the dog rose, which is more attractive than the more anaemic colour of the brier rose.

I wrote earlier in these notes that the cuckoo arrived in

early May and then was silent, but he has made up for it later. It has been a good year for cuckoos. When fishing last week at the Eye Brook Reservoir, the usual Eye Brook cuckoo was hard at work in the woods to the east. Nor was my day a blank for in the early evening I caught three beautiful trout of about two pound a-piece — one a brownie — on a large sunk orange fly. These fish were as pink as salmon on the table. I always smoke them in my Abu Smoker which takes about fifteen minutes per fish. Eaten cold with a fresh-cut lettuce and new potatoes they are really almost as good as sea trout.

As I played these fish to the net I speculated on the unseen monster which I lost the week before and never saw. There are a few really big fish in the Eye Brook reservoir, though not as large as those in Rutland Water, where (I was told) an enterprising piscator went round with an electric scanner and rapidly filled his bag before he was found out.

Trout fishing must never be 'made easy'. The more complicated the tackle the better, so it seems, though I must confess I am not a 'purist' and like to get my money's (and my patience) worth. All my fish were caught trolling on the drift, which to some is akin to shooting a sitting pheasant. The afternoon was still and humid with a curious mist, though there were just enough ripples to keep the fish moving.

The iris larvae have all pupated save three — amazingly early. The butterflies are due to emerge before the end of June — the earliest I ever remember. I put it down to the hot summer weather. They are at least a fortnight early and there should be eggs by mid-July, if not before. They were stripping the sallow in their net cage at such a pace I had to move thirteen of them to a new netted bush for they had begun to eat the leaves under which the early larvae had begun to pupate.

June 24

So the carp record has gone at last and that good fisherman Richard Walker will have to resign his crown! His fish was

44 lb. The new record is 51 lb. — a massive creature, beating Walker's by seven pounds no less! It came from Redmire — the same water which produced Walker's giant — a pool I know so well having fished it myself. Yet this stupendous fish — it was a mirror or scaleless carp, an ugly thing resembling a leather barrel — was certainly not the fish I once saw at Redmire, the vision of which has haunted me ever since.

I was fishing on the south bank — at a spot subsequently known as Pitchford's Pit, and something like a bronze rowing-boat materialized under the meadow sweet which fringed the pool. The water of Redmire is crystal clear and of considerable depth. This apparition was a fully scaled common carp clad in bronze mail, the huge scales overlapping like the rounded tiles on a roof.

Now a fish in the water always appears smaller than out of it and I am willing to swear that that carp topped 50 lb. and was nearer 70. I had never seen such a creature before — it was so vast it scared me. I suppose it was no more than a few inches below the surface in about three feet of water. It moved with the stealthy action of a stalking cat; it glided almost imperceptibly past my pitch — appearing like a mailed airship.

The history of this water — Redmire — (that is not its proper name) is somewhat wrapped in mystery. It is no more than two acres — perhaps a little over, and is surrounded by trees. At one end there is a wooded dingle where (when I fished there at nights) a savage bull grunted, roared, and threshed around.

It is an artificial pond, for at the western end is a stone dam which gives the appearance of great antiquity. One year I made a small oil painting of Redmire from the dam with the thick oaks lit by the evening sun reflected in the still dark water. I sent it to the Royal Academy, who accepted it but broke the frame so it was not hung.

The new record came from the top eastern end where the water was shallow and weedy and no doubt the 51 lb. fish was spawning there. I myself never took a fish from Redmire, though I came close to it on two occasions. Once when I had a floating crust out at the dam end I saw a big fish in the twenty-pound category lurking under some weeds nearby. I wooed him for two hours until he retired into the shadow of the weed. Becoming bored I walked along the bank to join a companion. Whilst idly chatting I heard what I took to be the harsh screech of a marauding jay, then realized it was a fish taking line off my reel. When I dashed round, most of the line was out to the backing, taut, into a vast weed bed. A careful pull on the line was answered by a swirl in the weeds. The hook broke.

Redmire is near the Welsh border, indeed one can see far to the west the blue loom of the Black Mountains. Both times I have been there the weather has been dull and cool. In the old boat house was a punt which was sadly in need of repair as its bottom boards were rotten. I mended it as best I could with copper nails and copper patches, so that it needed less bailing.

One evening later, when I was out on the bosom of the pool watching the light die behind the dark trees, I was aware of a faint bubbling sound which I at first thought to be a prowling carp. Then, to my horror, I saw that there was a strong bubbling spring at one end of the punt. We were sinking fast.

I had no bailer in the boat — in any case the water was coming in too fast to bail, and with a crazy home-made oar I made for the bank. It was a desperate dash. I was in over fifteen feet of water with plenty of weed tendrils, and with each forward movement the punt became more and more sluggish. I just made the shore when it sank under me.

It was a fascinating business cruising about over the deep water by the dam. The water was so clear (unusual in a carp water as they usually make a pond opaque with their routing in the muds) that you could see the slender tendrils of weed going down and down to be lost in peat-brown shadow. And everywhere the tiny silver seeds of the fresh water Daphnia shining like minute stars in an inky sky. Occasionally one glimpsed, far down, a burly mailed back as one of the big carps cruised under the punt.

The reason for the great weight attained by carp in

Redmire is the plentiful supply of 'plankton'; I believe they simply swim like whales with their mouths open.

I have just received an account of the capture of the 51 lb. fish from the fortunate piscator, Christopher Yates. He was fishing on the opening night of the coarse-fishing 1980 season at Redmire. The weather had been thundery which, curiously enough, is the best possible climate for catching great carp. Albert Buckby caught the first 'big' carp at Mapperley under these conditions — that was in 1930, but his fish, a 26-pounder, is now considered very run of the mill by Redmire standards, for this pool is, without doubt, Britain's premier carp water today. Here is Chris's description which I give with his kind permission:

> Last evening, I crept up to the shallows and, after an hour's fishing, discovered a small group of very big carp right at the top of the pool, where the stream flows in. After five casts, using two grains of corn on a size 8 and 9 lb. line weighted with plasticine, a huge fish took the bait 'on the drop'. The line tightened immediately and I struck into something that ran diagonally across the shallows, making a huge wave and a thunderous splash, that was heard right down at the far end of the pool. With the line brushing the sweeping branches of a willow that lay in the water to my left, I could do only one thing; I had to jump into the silt of the margin and flounder along to the right, the place where there used to be an old swans' nest; there I could manage things with a cooler head.
>
> I saw a big tail show above the surface — and then the carp bolted to the left and into the willow branch forty yards down the bank. With the rod low to the left and the handle bending, I rolled the fish off course and he came in towards me, but angling himself so that the pull on the line, and his thrusts, took him into the margins behind the willow tree I had tried to avoid (by jumping in)!
>
> I felt him slow, then stir. The line was touching the willow branches but I couldn't see any ripples spreading from behind them. To my horror, the fish began to 'creep'

along the margin, coming up to the tree. The line began to fall gently slack. Rapidly, I wound in and did the only thing that came to mind. I piled on all the pressure I dared, hoping to trick the fish into thinking I wanted it in the submerged tangle under the willow. It was a gamble, but it worked; the carp made a sudden lunge and dived off down the bank heading back towards the further willow. I stopped him with a yard or so to spare and then the carp just sulked, not pulling, nor attempting to sneak up to the tree in front of me. I'd shouted for help almost as soon as I hooked the fish and had jumped into the water, leaving my net behind me. But only when I was almost hoarse did one of my two companions answer. I'd thought that either they were asleep or else the evening breeze that was blowing up the lake was making it hard for them to hear.

At last, assistance arrived. But I didn't just want someone to wield the net, I needed someone to frighten the carp out from the margin, away from the difficult position between the two willows and into open water. Eventually, the third man appeared — climbing out into the half-submerged willow! There was a crack of a branch and the tree shook — but even before that, the fish had sensed the approach of number three and moved out. The line cut through the small ripples, angling steadily out into the middle of the shallows. There was a great plunging swirl which unfurled into a vast flat spot on the water. It reminded me of your description of the monster you lost at Beechmere — in your book *Confessions of a Carp Fisher*.

Pressure turned the beast over and he came arrowing straight towards us. I hardly needed to pull!

A large back slowly appeared above the surface as the carp moved into shallower and shallower water — and then, all went solid; the monster — for we could now see it was collosal — had beached itself in about nine inches of water!

My friend, John, squelched and sank into the silt as he worked his way nearer to the fish. I held on tight, keeping its head towards us as it tried to flip round, wallowing on its pectorals like some huge sea-monster about to draw itself up on to land. I could hardly dare to watch as John squeezed the net beneath the carp and tried to lift. This was the moment of truth, I thought, this is where it will explode out of the meshes and escape. It kicked once, but in doing so gave John a split second to get the net up. It was safe and I felt a great relief as the bend went out of the rod.

With much splashing and floundering, we both heaved the mud-covered bulk on to the grassy bank; there we washed its flanks with clean water and unhooked it — the hook-hold had been very fine, neatly in the corner of the bottom lip.

We three knelt in the soaking grass, looking down at a tremendous almost unbelievable mirror-carp. I ran for the big clock-scales, which go up to 60 lbs. and, in a large weighing bag, we hoisted the fish up, with two of us to lift it and hold the scales steady. I watched as I let the weight of the fish slowly down. The pointer crept round — past 40, past 45, past 50. I let my hands drop gently from the bottom of the bag and it hung free. The pointer read 51 lb. 14 oz.!

The bag weighed 8 oz. The fish was 51 lb. 6 oz. The moon hung low in the afterglow. The evening was suddenly very still — or at least seemed so — as we three looked at each other.

I know that top corner of Redmire so well for I have sat under the willows on sunny evenings and watched dim elongated shapes gliding about in the shallow water. No doubt they find good feed there where the stream flows into the pool.

To see these elusive monsters cruising about, sometimes with their hump backs breaking surface, was tremendously frustrating, and exciting too — they seemed so unattainable and secure.

Yates's fish resembled one of those harvest barrels which the old-time reapers took to the fields when they cut the corn — rotund, very deep. It measured $36\frac{1}{2}$ inches from fork to tail with a girth of $34\frac{1}{2}$ inches; an ugly object as all mirrors

118

are, quite unlike the full scaled carp, in their bronze and plated mail.

June 29 ————————————————————————————

I laid a screwdriver with a rounded handle on the bonnet of my car today whilst doing a job on my drive gate.

A brisk wind was blowing. I noticed the screwdriver was describing a circle — each gust of wind smiting the rounded handle making it describe a circular motion so that it was in no danger of falling off. It occurred to me that the guillemot's egg on the cliff ledge did exactly that, rotating on its axis and not falling off. Now how in the name of wonder did nature in its wisdom so form the egg — large and rounded at one end and tapering off to a point?

I can understand a living creature adapting to its environment and developing in a way which preserved its existence but how could a 'lifeless' thing like an egg decide to be the exact shape? Certainly the bird could never have thought out the puzzle of how to keep its egg from falling off the ledge.

There are truly wonders in nature which remain a mystery unless some Designer figures out these problems! And here is another mystery of nature. How does the bumble bee fly with that heavy rotund body and small frail wings? Even modern high speed photography can give no clue. If we could solve the secret, man might be able to fly under his own power with equal ease.

Which reminds me that my swallow family in my studio are almost ready for the great adventure. Five of them are now so cramped in the nest they have to perch on one another, and within the next twenty-four hours they should leave the nest.

All day long the parents come with flies — every three minutes or so, all through the long day. They always follow the same route — round the old apple trees at the top of the garden, then, with a graceful curvy glide, sweep round by the french windows and up into the studio. If this brood gets off safely they will most likely decide to have a second brood and I shall be barred from my studio until they fly at summer's end.

The cuckoo was calling today in the forest — it may be it is the last time I shall hear it this year, so quickly do the days race by.

The wayside flowers have gone to seed already — only the stout coarse hog weeds raise their putty coloured umbrellas and the elder is in its full flowering. Even the lime trees are getting ready to bloom. What a heavenly scent that is — the last true scent of summer!

It is a perfume which affects me powerfully, for it brings back memories of early manhood when I was studying in London at the Royal College of Art — shut away from the quiet fields. But at the end of July the holidays began — just at the time of the lime flowering.

We had four or five noble limes overlooking the gravel sweep to Lamport Rectory where I was born. The lime scent was something to look forward to. Woodpigeons always nested in the trees and their croonings and cooings roused me from sleep in the early mornings.

My father was a keen radio fan — long before television was invented, and he persuaded a bold village lad to climb to the top of the tallest tree to fix a pole there. From this tall tree an aerial stretched across to another tall tree on the croquet lawn — an American oak.

It was an adventurous day when the aerial was fixed and we were able to listen to the Savoy bands in London, never dreaming that one day we should both see and hear, and in natural colours, events taking place thousands of miles distant.

One autumn day I spied a fat woodpigeon sitting among the saffron-coloured October leaves of the middle tree. Ever a bloodthirsty youth, I fetched my ·22 rifle and, taking steady aim, brought the bird down in a cloud of feathers.

Even as I fired I realized that the East window of my father's church was exactly in line. At next Sunday's service a furtive glance revealed a small round hole high in the coloured glass.

120

My father never noticed it. I suppose the hole still remains. One day I must go and see.

June 30

The female moorhen has been away from the garden for over a week, though the male attends each morning.

The reason for this absence of his lady love was revealed to me this morning as I walked up the road. Something black caught my eye in the tangled grass. It was the unfortunate hen.

She was always a wandering restless soul — extremely nervous, so unlike her mate. A pity! I shall not see those little blackamoors after all this season, unless he can find another mate. But the summer draws on, and already the farmer has set a 'banger' going in the ripening corn over the road.

I cannot understand why moorhens — normally such shy secretive birds and well capable of flight, should fall victims to the motorist. Blackbirds are stupid enough, but the moorhen is more often hit by passing cars. And every year I see them lying dead in the roads. Yellow hammers also seem only half awake and allow a car to be almost on them before stirring.

At this time of year — around midsummer — the carrion crows and magpies wax fat on the furred and feathered victims hit by cars, a lazy way of earning a living. You will never run over a magpie or crow even when it is busy on a carcase — I have yet to see either of these cunning birds killed in this way, though owls are sometimes killed at night when devouring road carrion.

Even the lithe and active stoat and weasel are seen lying dead, as are rats and rabbits and many a hare. The latter become quite confused in car lights and are easily run down for they have not the sense to dart aside out of the brilliant beam. Each summer a heavy toll is taken of fledgling birds — especially pheasants, partridges, and green plover — for in wet weather their parents bring them out into the road to dry off. I once

121

came upon a hen pheasant brooding her full compliment of babies in the middle of a country road after a heavy shower. Wet weather is a deadly enemy of ground-nesting game birds for their feathers are not sufficiently water-proofed like those of ducks and geese.

July 3 ———————————————————

The young swallows in the studio flew this
morning, after being weather bound for
three days by high winds, miserable rain, and
anxious parents.

The morning dawned fine and warm. So
the great adventure began. What excitement! On uncertain
wings they sped about the garden, coming to fluttering rest on
the high sprays of the willow by Big Pond. What a joyous day
indeed for both the five youngsters and myself! To find themselves airborne in a paradise of light, air, and sunshine — what
a change from the shadows of my studio!

All day they flitted about like butterflies, every minute
feeling more secure, resting now and then on the willows when
feeble wings became weary, watched over solicitously by their
devoted parents. In the evenings they returned to the nest for
early sleep.

Few young birds return to the nest so lately left — moorhens do so, but I can think of no other birds save owls and
kestrels. Tits never return to their nest once they have left it.
Unlike young swallows, they can fend for themselves straight
away, scattering to all parts of the landscape. All the finch
family leave home for good.

As yet, those young swallows cannot be aware of any
danger in this paradise. Their sheer delight is obvious. This
magical scene before them, the sunlit trees — the blue sky, the
leaves turning and gleaming in the summer winds, is their
inheritance. This so suddenly, and in so short a time! And
now, for this night, and many nights — until the parents drive
them off to another brood, the studio nest will still be a
haven — warmth at night and security from peril.

For a few of them — not all — there is a wonderful exist-

123

ence in store — the excitement of summer's end, and then the great urge which will soon possess them to fly away to distant lands very different from this quiet garden.

With what wistful sadness shall I see them go — I, chained by my weight, a prisoner of the laws of gravitation, as earthbound as a beetle!

The saga of my moorhen guests continues. Once again the cock bird is a widower after his two abortive attempts to raise a family. Each day he haunts the ponds, coming each morning to be fed — calling at times for his lost mate, as he did in the spring time. Perhaps he will find another lady of more mature years and bring her to the garden and introduce her to the ponds, for he is loath to leave us.

The cuckoo still calls but the wheat is tall and green — the hedgerow trees dark and bosky, the colour used by the old water-colour masters, De Windt and Cotman.

Secret corners of the garden which, in winter, are bare and open, are now sinister caves of shadow, forming ambuscades for cats and rats, overhung with nettles and elder, a miniature, sinister, tropical forest. The tremendous bursting surge of life is now at full flood. It is difficult to keep pace with all the hedge cutting and grass mowing which is necessary at this time.

The pupae of the purple emperors hang from their sallow leaves, still a tender green. It needs sun to bring them on to the day of release. For them, like the young swallows, there will be a glorious emergence into the sunlit forest, but only for a brief moment — a mere twenty-eight days or so.

So all this teeming life is eternal for as long as the sun glows warmth and energy. Even if we wipe out our own existence prematurely through evil folly, it will go on without us for many million years, when it will gradually fade away as the earth cools, or, because of some cosmic explosion, will be snuffed out in a merciful instant of time.

But the swallows will yet return for springs beyond counting. Even though our share of existence, if measured by time, is infinitely more brief than the life of a mayfly let us make the most of it 'while life lasts'. After all — we only have

124

one span on trust. Like wealth (money wise) 'you can't take it with you' unless — like the butterfly we emerge into a yet more wonderful existence.

July 6

At last I have been able to witness the miracle of a purple emperor's emergence from the chrysalis.

Strange as it may seem, over the years when I have bred these lovely creatures for conservation, I have never been on hand to see the butterfly at the time of emergence. But today — (an afternoon of warm gloom and little sun) I happened to visit the breeding cage and was just in time to see the suspended chrysalis in violent motion. It split asunder. Out crawled the emperor — a bloated greenish-white body with two crumpled coloured knobs on its back, appearing quite a frightening monstrosity as hideous as a dragon-fly larvae.

It was careful not to fall from the suspended casing as it sensed the pull of gravitation. One slip, and if it fell, those wings would never expand to their full extent and would remain deformed. There was a moment of rather desperate clawing, then it reached the tip of the chrysalis and hung exhausted.

Now the magic took place before my eyes.

Those crumpled, coloured knobs unfolded as I watched like those Japanese flowers which expand in water which I remember playing with as a boy. The hind wings expanded first, then the forewings. These took longer to stiffen and fill out, but within a quarter of an hour from the time of emergence they were perfect. One could not imagine how so large an insect could have been packed away in so small a container.

Those wings were like a folded parachute — very cunningly folded too — and were now blossoming forth. The insect remained passive thereafter, hanging from the tip of the chrysalis. Once the wings parted briefly to reveal a blaze of iridescent purple, but were quickly closed.

Three others emerged shortly after — all males — though I was not there to witness it. By late afternoon I released them in the reserve ten miles distant.

Watching that miracle of nature, so exquisite and performed with such delicacy, I remembered how a year ago — in a hot riding — I found the eggs in the 'Sally gardens'; how I hatched them and saw the larvae grow until the winds and rains of winter sent them into their long winter sleep. I had a sense of triumph at the fulfilment of my efforts — this was the moment of truth both for me and them. I have still fifteen more to hatch and cannot leave home until all are safely released.

As to the swallow family — my other precious feathered children — they have safely flown but return each night for sleep in the old nest. Their parents — feeling no doubt a sense of triumph and satisfaction as to the outcome have, believe it or not, begun another nest alongside the first! For the last two days they have been hard at work. I notice they are utilising a nail as a support system.

There is a semi-circle of mud and grass behind the nail which is equidistant from either 'horn' of mud, and the back is being built up to cover the nail.

So this means I shall still have once again to vacate my studio to my guests; I cannot see getting to work again in there for at least another month! This will bring us to early August when (I hope) the swallows will have been satisfied and will relinquish their lease. In my garage also I have a nest which necessitates covering my car each night with dust sheets, otherwise the paint work is covered with white spots.

But bless their little bottoms, I say — no swallow will ever ask for my hospitality in vain, I would have them in my bedroom if they wished to come and they could bombard my counterpane to their bums' content!

July 9————————————————————————

Surely this is the most melancholy July for many years — days of wind and rain and very cool.

126

I took up a male iris to the Chase this afternoon and put it on the leeside of the fir where I put two others yesterday — a male and female. To my astonishment I found them in exactly the same place — they had not moved. Their wings were shut. This shows how this butterfly will remain in shelter during inclement weather when in the wild.

The males I released two days ago, when the sun shone, sped away over the oak tops with that speed of flight which rivals any other of our British butterflies. If the dour weather continues I doubt if the breeding season will be a good one, but there is time yet.

In my studio the swallows' new nest is three-quarters completed and the young of the former brood come back each night to the old nest.

July 14 —————————————————————

A crisis! The second nest built by the studio swallows has partially collapsed. One side was built round a nail for support but the unsupported side came away from the wall so that the whole nest was tilted.

Luckily she hadn't begun to lay. I fixed a beam, cut to size and jammed between the two walls for support but I do not think this has proved popular. They sense the nest is insecure, as it has come away from the wall, and I doubt if they will go on with their work. When I peeped in late last night just before ten p.m. the family was back and roosting.

This dreadful July — surely the coldest, wettest July of the century! Here we are at mid-month and no sun to speak of, though on the thirteenth I took to the Reserve four more purple emperors — two males and two females and released them during a brief spell of sunlight. They flew away strongly over the oak tops.

If the dreadful cold wet sunless days continue I cannot see how they will breed, for their time is restricted and they must have warmth and sun to become active. This morning — in the grey east wind after a night of continuous cold rain, the martins and swallows were hawking up and down in the lee of the oaks, swifts with them.

Soon these latter birds will be away to Africa — their sojourn here is only a brief nine weeks or so. What strange birds these are whose whole life is spent on the wing — sleeping, eating and mating!

I have never seen swifts drink like the swallows and martins, though of course they are a different race, more akin to the night-jars. Yet, if the swallow tribe need to drink why not the swifts? Perhaps night-jars never drink — that I do not know.

July 16

The swallow family in my studio have apparently appreciated my efforts to save and support the tilted nest for the mother swallow is now sitting on eggs.

July 22

Returning to Northamptonshire from that *crème de la crème* of our English countryside, Hampshire, I was struck by the contrast between those soft wooded hills and valleys and the plain 'homely' look of the Midland fields, hardly enhanced now by the stark dead poles of diseased elms — scores of them standing in bleached white nakedness amongst the hedges.

Little wonder W. H. Hudson loved Hampshire — he was, I think, happier there than anywhere since his boyhood or the pampas of South America.

I had gone to the New Forest to see the filming of my book *Brendon Chase* which has been filming for six months — unhappily the worst summer for very many years. Yet when I was there the sun shone, the Forest was at its best with the bright sunlight making coins of golden light on the Forest floor revealing delightful vistas between the great oaks. A feature of the New Forest — one which I had not noted before — was the abundance of holly, sometimes forming miniature spinneys within the great canopy of beech and oaks around them.

As daughter Angela and I walked down through the Forest to the location, a bright red adder, with black back markings, wound its way across the track within a few inches of us. It was the first red adder I have seen, others have always been the blue or blue-green variety. There used to be an old saying that the red variety had a more deadly bite. This of course must be nonsense. It did not hurry — indeed at one point it stopped and looked about. It was a small one — possibly a male.

Later I visited a large forest in the area. The afternoon was excessively hot and the wide riding, bordered by oaks and (I fear) newly planted wretched conifers, lay under the blistering sun. Many commas were on the wing and one silver-washed fritillary. At one point a grove of rather coarse-leaved sallows fringed the path, backed by tall oaks. As we approached, a magnificent female purple emperor flew out of the sallow close by and was gone in a moment with that swift purposeful flight which is even more swift than that of the fritillaries. Later a male swooped and soared over the tops of the sallows. The flight is unmistakable — they glide like partridges — the wings outspread showing the black bands.

What a sight to see! this rare and magnificent butterfly — the only 'tropical' butterfly on the British list — swooping and soaring in the hot sunlight!

I met a collector with a large green net and had a long and interesting conversation with him. I asked him why it was that the males emerged first. I told him that out of twenty-three I brought through the winter for release eighteen were males which all hatched first. He was of the opinion that they are like the migrating birds which, when they first arrive in this country, all are males, the idea being that they 'stake out' their territories before the arrival of their ladies. This may well be so.

130

On this date as I write (July 22) I still have one remaining chrysalis to hatch. It is still green and has not darkened. Just prior to emergence the three or four creases on the envelope are seen to widen and glisten. When this occurs, emergence takes place in the matter of an hour or so, but the actual emergence is not often seen for the whole business takes less than three minutes.

A large and tangled wood where the black hairstreak is known to be found seemed worth a visit as the morning was hot and still. It was something of a relief to leave the burning field, to enter into the cool cloisters of oak and thorn. Flies jigged in the shade under the arching tunnel of trees. Beyond was a brilliantly lit clearing full of all manner of weeds and wild flowers including the beautiful delicate pink mallow, willow herb, teazle, and crumbly cream flowers of the meadow sweet.

Meadow sweet, that true flower of the quiet field headland attracts the black hairstreak, but I looked in vain for this sombre and elusive insect — one of our rarest, rarer even than the purple emperor. I remembered the day long ago when I saw a privet bush in a Northamptonshire forest alive with black hairstreaks. At that time I did not even know they were a rare species!

It is on the wing in June, so I suspect I was too late. Even so, the sunless wet July might — I hope — have delayed emergence.

The sunlit clearing smelled deliciously of hot damp vegetation — a real midsummer smell, but the only butterflies on the wing were ringlets and hedgebrowns — a drab company. Turtle doves purred, woodpigeons cooed and a nightingale sounded its alarm note 'wee purr, wee purr'. There are at least three pairs in this wood, where a few years ago there were more than double that number.

Though my search was fruitless I found solace in that scented sunlit glade with its bright wild flowers with the background lullaby of the turtle doves.

131

August 1 _____

My beloved little 'hen wife', my hen
bullfinch, is dead, all through my
own folly which makes it all the more
tragic.

Seven years ago I rescued her from a drowned-out nest.
Her eyes were barely open and the quills just showing blue on
her skinny little body. Over the years she has been my best-
loved pet. She was devoted to me, having a fixation on me as I
was her foster parent, so much so that she showed no sexual
interest in my two cock bullies, though they had plenty to say
to her.

She would take a hemp seed from my lips and pull my hair
and look into my eyes with her little brown ones. She would
bend in the middle with sweet twitterings to ask me to mount
her. All this will sound nonsense to many people but there was
an almost spiritual bond between us. She would give me a great
welcome if I had been absent and scold me too, meowing like a
little cat.

A few days ago I noticed she was listless and puffed out —
her eyes small, the wings held out at an angle, a deadly sign.
Then she slept with head into wing, the feathers puffed out so
that she resembled a little fluffy ball. Cold death was near.

I knew then the end was close and wracked my brains as to
the cause.

Could it be that she was egg bound? But there was no sign
of that — if she was I could have helped her by steaming her
little stern over a cup of boiling water and gentle application of
olive oil. On the afternoon of the thirtieth she died.

On looking through some old diaries I found an entry
about another hen I lost. NO PLANTAIN SEED. And with
horror I remembered I had given her some plantain seed the

other day — a long stalk of giant plantain, unripe. That was the cause. Bullfinches will eat dried plantain seed, but not when it is green.

This tragedy has left me with a slow ache of sorrow — it will be some time before it leaves me. How is it that a tiny being like this can so wind itself about my heart?

Another upsetting thing occurred last week. All the fish in my Big Pond were floating belly up — including the big carp I put in from the lake at my old home. Again my fault.

The pond has not been cleaned out for five years and the accumulation of years of autumn leaves have so fouled the water that even the carp — a fish which can live in the muddiest pond — failed to survive. The whole surface of the pool was covered with the white 'belly up' fish ranging from roach and dace to tiny fingerlings bred in the pool. So at autumn's end the pond must be pumped out — in what manner I have yet to decide for it will be a formidable undertaking.

Somehow it hasn't been my week. The only bright spot is the swallow family in my studio — the second instalment. She is sitting on infant young. The beam I fixed under the tilted nest has done its job.

August 3

Oppressive August heat, the air lifeless and already signs of stubble burning on far horizons. The sky luminous, hot looking, thunder working up.

Along the narrow track this morning the grasses were gay with gatekeepers and hedgebrowns — those russet-coloured butterflies, humble plodders of the roadside margins. There must have been a big hatch. It is a species more common in the south country than the Midlands.

Like the purple emperor it hibernates in the larva state among the winter grass. The bright fulvous brown shows up quite vividly as it flits about the herbage on which it lays its minute eggs.

Like the meadow brown, ringlet, and wall, it is what I call a lower middle-class butterfly. Those I saw were rejoicing in the windless heat which I found almost suffocating. Few other species were on the wing, only the odd green-veined white, few meadow browns, and no small coppers or blues. Blackberry blossoms showed in the wild untamed hedge and the hedge browns were busy over these — in the old days this lane would have been busy with tortoiseshells, peacocks, and all the 'hedgerow' butterflies — the blues and the coppers.

I came to an ancient tumbledown gate and looked out over a vast field — one of my 'quiet fields'. It was typical of this Midland county — it looked as inhospitable and uninteresting as an African veld, stretching away to the far headland and its dimly seen high hawthorn hedge.

The very 'ordinariness' of this vast field fascinated me — it was a field one would never find in Hampshire. And yet it held me with a certain fascination, for it reminded me of boyhood evening stalks at rabbits in the late summer holidays, when I bellied my way between thistle clumps and ant hills as cautiously as any red-deer stalker.

This field held thistles too — and nettle clumps. An old stone drinking trough was near the gate, the earth around it cracked all over like the forehead of an old man, with fine lines. Spiders ran there — crickets shrilled, the heated air danced over the flowering thistle heads.

There was a fine peacock visiting the thistle heads, it looked as large and dark as a purple emperor. It was methodical in its search for nectar. But no other life was visible — no birds to see or hear — just this vast thistle-grown field shimmering in the August heat.

I know the green plover breed there in spring, among the ant hills, but they were absent today — hatched, flown and gone. Perhaps out there among the thistles there was a partridge with her brood — there would certainly be hares snugged down in their forms, ears flat on the shoulders, brown eyes half closed in the languorous heat.

It was the sort of field which made one feel tired at the

thought of tramping across it, with the first thistle spines working their way into one's socks.

Even when you reached the far hedge there would be little of interest, for it has not been laid for half a century and is in reality a line of close-crowding hawthorns. But the cattle have forced their way through — there is no headland wire. As a hedge to retain stock it is useless. And beyond that hedge? Yet another great quiet field, thistle grown and remote with no sheep or cattle pasturing there.

Yet these thistly deserts sometimes provide great interest to the field naturalist.

Some years ago I found a colony of painted ladies had adopted a lonely pasture, such a one as this, and the caterpillars had spun their web tents among the spined leaves. I have never since found painted ladies breeding. I rested my arms on the top bar of the gate and stared across the great field hoping to see at least some movement of pigeon or crow.

The peacock butterfly passed from sight, leaving that great 'still' field drowsing in the August heat, weary with Summer.

The swallows in my studio have deserted the second nest. When I climbed up I found one minute dead chick lying among the feathered lining. They will not nest again but perhaps next spring they will return. At least they have produced one fine brood. They should have been content with that.

August 9 ————————————————————————

To my astonishment the swallow pair in the studio have decided to build yet again — this time nearer the window on the chimney breast! This seems to be a much more workman-like effort but I cannot see how the young will be fit enough to fly on migration.

Each night when I look into the studio I see the devoted

couple sitting on the nest rim facing each other. (I do not think they have eggs as yet.)

They are early to bed — by eight p.m. whilst other birds in the garden are active — but by four a.m. they are out and about in the grey dawn sitting on the willow by Big Pond or outside my bedroom window on the telephone wires.

To me there was something touching about that bird and wife — two little wedded beings who are living out their brief span and fulfilling their destinies — rearing their young and passing on the torch of warm life to another generation.

And if all goes well the same pair will be back after their adventurous wanderings — to build again in my studio nest spring. The previous brood are nowhere to be seen and I wonder if they have already left these shores for Africa. They certainly do not roost on the premises — in my studio or the garage.

In this the swallow differs from the longtailed tits who keep their young with them right through the winter to another spring.

Once the swallow young are active and able to fend for themselves they are banished from the family home and made to face the wide world.

I paid a visit recently to a fine private wood in Berkshire, having had kind permission from the owner who guards it jealously against 'collectors'. I have never seen a more perfect setting for Iris — huge oak trees of really majestic proportions and wide clearings and ridings fringed with sallow.

This year in my Reserve the sallows have been diseased and eaten. Only four eggs have been gathered and those after hours of patient searching. But in this fine wood the sallows were for the most part healthy and green, though the day, typical of the wretched summer of 1980, was dour and damp with an atmosphere like that of a greenhouse.

Halfway down the wide main ride stood a gigantic oak, a real Emperor Tree round which the males play in the August heats. And on the fresh green sallows below Angela found seven newly laid eggs — pale blue in colour — a great triumph. I could only find one solitary egg. All were laid in the tall sallows which we could only reach down with the aid of my crook. This struck me as unusual as most are laid in the sallows on the lower inner boughs.

The wood was very dense in places with rides cutting through the undergrowth — few firs, which Iris abhors — and mostly oaks and ash. Everywhere the trodden paths of deer and at the ride junctures were high seats for deer shooters.

On a day of sun the main ride would be a marvellous vantage point to see Iris but even on a suitable day it is rarely glimpsed, and the purple glory of the male's wings takes place some sixty feet from the ground.

August 12

I have solved a question which has long been in my mind — why the purple emperor is so rare. When the infant larva hatches it eats its egg case and retires to the peak of its seat leaf, going down to the very tip where it turns around with its black head facing the leaf. This is a purely defensive action against predators, the chief of which is a very small pied beetle whose Latin name, I have ascertained from an expert, is *Anthocoris nemorum*. (Another protecting feature for Iris, when it is very small, is the rain drop which drains down the 'gutter' of the leaf and completely encloses the larva.)

When I looked in at my rearing cage today at a newly hatched larva I saw it being savagely attacked by one of these minute beetles. Before I could kill it it had bitten the larva in two. Now, the sallows in the woods are infested with this small and savage beetle which must account for *thousands* of newly hatched larvae in August. When the larva grows larger it is better able to combat this vicious little predator, though of course it is no match for the other chief predators — earwigs — spiders and ladybirds.

No wonder then that the butterfly is so scarce! This

discovery of mine, I am sure, should be of great interest to all entomologists.

The beetle is most elusive and difficult to capture. This one I sent for identification by an expert at Monks Wood Research Station was only captured by the use of my 'tickling stick'. This consists of a slender rod, the tip of which is dipped in grease. The creature is caught on this and is held fast. It is the way I combat predators in my rearing cages — earwigs and spiders are quickly disposed of by this method.

The interesting fact is that the beetle, once interested in the destruction of its prey, is very 'one-track minded' and will attack the larva as savagely as a wolf or tiger. When not so engaged it is wary and evasive, dodging round leaf buds and angles of twigs. The earwig — if alarmed — very sensibly drops off the leaf or twig at the first hint of danger, and spiders also will drop off. Some larvae of moths and butterflies and wood-lice also adopt this method of escape, rolling up and dropping off. The larvae of Iris never do so.

When one considers the vast numbers of these various predators on a single forest bush of sallow it is a wonder that any Iris survive to pupation. Even when pupated and hanging from the underside of a leaf they are attacked. Lately I have found Iris pupae in the wild with just the peak of the chrysalis attached to the underside of the sallow leaf, the rest, missing, having been devoured — possibly by birds as well as other creatures.

Not long ago I found a fully grown larva of the puss moth on a sallow. I brought this home — a fine handsome object with its fearsome grotesque mask which is enough to scare birds from attacking it. I put it on a sallow in my garden and visited it daily to see how it was progressing.

One afternoon I found it half eaten. The predator was on an adjoining leaf — an impressive bright green creature which is far from common in the Midlands — the great green bush cricket (*Tettigona viridissima*) 5 c.m. long. No larvae of a moth, butterfly, eggs, or pupae is safe from this creature which can make short work of earwigs or spiders.

One would have thought that Iris, being so subject to the attention of predators, would lay large quantities of eggs to compensate for the loss. Yet a female Iris lays less than two hundred eggs — one hundred and thirty to one hundred and fifty is supposed to be the maximum and these are always laid singly, usually one or two to a bush, never in a cluster like those of the tortoiseshells, peacocks, and red admirals. These caterpillars protect themselves by weaving webs, though this does not deter ichneumon flies.

The latter apparently does not attack the larvae of Iris. The large tortoiseshell, possibly one of our rarest butterflies today with the exception of the large blue, was especially prone to the attentions of ichneumon flies, whose method of ensuring the continuance of their species is one of the darker and less pleasant ways of nature. It lays its eggs in the body of a caterpillar which is then eaten alive by the larvae when they hatch, a horrible arrangement.

Hunting wasps will also take larvae. As I described in an earlier book, *The Naturalist's Bedside Book*, I saw a wasp, flying past a willow leaf, suddenly 'back track' and bite the head off a small puss-moth caterpillar which I had under observation. The incident was dramatic and sudden. The wasp flew off with the head and the body dropped to the ground.

August 16 ————————————————————————

Harker's Brook is a modest Midland stream. It flows at the bottom of the village under the old stone bridge, the haunt of kingfisher and moorhen and delicate damosell dragonflies in high summer.

On hot days in late May I have leant over the stone coping which is rough with moss and coloured rusty lichen, engraved with the initials of long-dead rustics, and watched the minnows and gudgeon spawning on the sandy bottom beyond the water forget-me-nots. In the dog days the cattle stand knee deep with their thick-lashed eyes half closed. Higher up, away from the hamlet, gaunt grey herons stalk in the willow shade.

On the night of August 14, 1980, I was awakened in the early hours by the steady drum of a stupendous downpour. Thunder shook the house — sudden white blazes of lightning lit Far Forest, instantaneously, as light as noon day, quicker than the blink of an eye.

Three inches of rain fell upon us that night. Next morning Harker's Brook appeared still unconcerned. Some twelve hours later it exploded. The whole valley went under, and marvellous vistas opened out.

Chicken coops among the nettles by the Rectory fence arose and bobbed about — dogs stood on kennel tops, corn fields disappeared. Behind the Rectory a vast lake appeared, miraculously improving the landscape beyond all recognition, as though some Capability Brown had been at work.

Ornamental ponds, lately stocked (expensively) with golden orfe and exotic lilies, vanished from view and the fish fled joyfully down to the distant river where, no doubt, they will in time cause great astonishment to patient coarse fishermen when they pull in their worm bait. The widow Deeks stood apprehensively at her doorstep watching the brown flood creep even higher until it washed the very step on which she stood. The village was as disturbed as an overturned beehive.

Police arrived in thigh waders, two venturesome cars were marooned, sitting sullenly in the flood with their drivers imprisoned within. Nobody remembered such a flood since 1912.

It was a flood which will no doubt be the subject of tavern talk in the neighbourhood for many years. The only inhabitants of the village who showed any enthusiasm were the white ducks at the Manor Farm, who were as joyous as children in new fallen snow.

Together with two ancient men I leant upon the wall of the old bridge watching the sudden heave and surge of the brown water against the arch, wondering if a huge tree trunk, later felled in the miller's meadow, would attempt a passage of

141

the bridge. It was held by a single strand of barbed wire, while the flood foamed about it endeavouring to push it free. Then in an hour, or less, the water drained away, the floating hen coops with their unfortunate drowned inhabitants went aground on the nettles, the dogs descended from their kennel tops, and Harker's Brook was almost normal once more. Only the great tree trunk remains on the flat meadow hard up against the strand of barbed wire.

The white ducks trooped back to the farm wagging their white sterns and flapping their wings at intervals — it had been a wonderful experience for them — and for us.

August 20

It seemed only last week that I stood on the headland by the old oak tree watching the combine harvester cutting this field. Twelve months have passed and here I am again! The swift passage of time fills me with unease, and this summer of 1980 has been one of the most gloomy and wet on record. Yet now the sun shone with power, a hot stiff west wind stirred the oak overhead, hissing and fluttering in the dark green leaves where a few pale acorns showed, food for questing pheasants in the coming October days. It was a wind which had no refreshing coolness in it — a desert wind.

In front of me the field sloped down to the valley and the Manor farm, with its old stone barns where white pigeons wheeled. To these barns all that day the tractor-towed wagons had been piled high with a rich harvest of wheat. As soon as one left the field another came jolting over the stubble to take its place.

The bulk of the field had been cut — now, only a block of standing corn remained, a neat oblong golden 'box' of wheat, the heavy heads of their short straws bowing to the wind.

The great lumbering harvester, which shook the very earth, as big as a cottage with its shuttling knives, toiled up and down, a lurching monster trailing a cloud of dust which blew sideways on the wind. Henry, the driver, was perched high on his seat, like a 'mahout' on the neck of an elephant, a mask about his face to protect him from the dust. This man has a strange history. He is a German and was once a prisoner of war. He married an English girl from the village. He has almost forgotten his native tongue, his children cannot speak it, and is a fine big man, the best workman on the farm, and the most reliable.

Seen afar off the harvester does not seem to move — only the blowing dust and the faint rumble tells of its inexorable passage. On either side of this ever-narrowing block of corn, the cut swathes lie in thick bolsters of straw, all parallel one to the other with a space of bristly cut stubble between the rows.

As I stood in the shade of the oak with Polar my labrador beside me, I looked along the edge of the cut corn watching for a hare. When the combine harvester had regurgitated its stream of golden grain into the empty belly of the trailer at the far end of the field and swung round to start its upward journey once more, I saw a hare come out of the standing corn opposite, pause a moment, then run across the open space to the roll of straw into which it crept with flattened ears. I marked the spot and walked quietly down with my gun at the ready. But the hare was not there, though the dog snuffed about and I kicked the straw.

Then I realized the cunning animal had passed *through* the straw, and, keeping low with flattened ears, had departed down the cut stubble unseen by me. Hares will always do this in a harvest field. The roll of straw is at least a foot high, this gives plenty of cover.

I had to get back to my post by the oak without delay as the grumbling harvester was already halfway up the standing strip, the chaff blowing sideways in a cloud.

Fred Johnson — dead-eye Dick — was guarding the far corner on the opposite side. As I hurried to the tree I saw him raise his gun. There was a fractional pause. The shot ran out. I saw him send his black retriever for a hare.

Now the thunder of the combine was loud, the shuttling knives, working like those clippers at the hairdressers, were scything through the dry straight stems. Then they were hoisted clear, the metal giant swung round, and started back on its return journey.

Only a thirty yard width of corn remained. If any creature was crouching there it must have been in fear profound at that vibrating rumble coming ever nearer. Far off beyond the farm buildings the horizon was misted with the stubble burning — golden fields stretched as far as the eye could see, the trees muffled and blue. A swallow went coursing by, singing exultantly. The rumbling grew fainter. No other hares came out my side, but another offered Fred a chance as the reaper made its last ascent of the field. This rolled over to the shot.

The last strip of standing crop, not ten feet through, was severed by the shuttling blades. Now the field will dream in the autumn scene for a little while. Partridges will run the stubbles and the odd pheasant in the early day will come quietly on the headland by the old oak tree. Then will come the plough and the dark earth, white gulls, and peewits. All the leaves will fly from the oak to lie in the troughs found by the plough share, sodden, buff, and red.

It was an autumn scene which has a familiar delight for me. It mattered not that I had not slain a hare. No doubt the one Fred gave me will, in due time, be relished, with a dash of port wine and red currant jelly, a real Harvest Hare. This wild child of the upand fields (which, unlike man, had no knowledge of death as his destiny) knew not what slew him, so mercifully and swiftly, that golden afternoon.

I went on down to Bob's 'wild pasture' which he sets aside for butterflies and wild life. All manner of weeds flourish there, thistles in profusion, their gossamer-white crowns lifting to the wind, and purple spines of rosebay willow herb among the crowding sallows.

Painted ladies flew here, delicately coloured butterflies, pink, white, black, and orange in delightful harmony. No doubt they bred on the thistles, for the spiny black and green larvae feed on them, each apart and wearing for itself a silken tent to keep out evil-doers.

144

I once searched a 'quiet field' which held many thistles, and found many of those silken tents each tenanted by a caterpillar of a painted lady therein. I took some and bred them to the complete butterfly. It is a lovely insect — the outside of its wings are more subtly coloured than the inside, with whorls of greenish marbling suffused with a glorious glow of pink near the shoulder of the forewing.

I wondered, as I watched one sidling on a flowering thistle, why butterflies have such beautifully coloured wings. The reason has nothing to do with camouflage, for what could be more vivid than the black and bright red-orange of the red admiral, or the purple flush of the purple emperor? It cannot be to attract the opposite sex, although in many butterflies the colouring of the male is brighter.

Camouflage certainly plays a part in a butterfly like the grayling, which, visible enough in flight, seems to vanish when it settles. Tortoiseshells and peacocks scarcely differ in colouring, in this they resemble the kingfisher and the goldfinch amongst birds — the sexes are equally colourful. Certainly in birds the male is usually the brighter. This must surely be to attract the female, the most striking instance being the birds of paradise when the female is invariably dowdy and drab.

It would seem then that the kingfisher and goldfinch do not need colour to attract the female. Others do, birds such as the ruff and blackcock, capercailzie, pheasant, bullfinch and chaffinch, though the reason may be that the 'dam' (as old Gilbert White terms the female of a species) has to be soberly clad when brooding her young.

Jays and magpies have no fear of predators other than man so the sexes are similar, no creature would seek to try conclusions with those wicked bills.

August 25 ————————————————————

When I put Polar, my labrador, to bed tonight I met a hedgehog in the path. He had evidently been sampling the crumbs of dog biscuit in Polar's pen.

Our meeting was sudden but not unfriendly. He (I think it was a 'he' but sexing hedgehogs is dodgy) did not roll up into a ball but paused with snout extended and a slightly astonished look in his little piggy eye. Hedgehogs are not all that common in my garden though there are dense shrubberies and trim lawns for nightly worm hunting. Maybe it is the same pig, now mature, which I put in the garden two years since, a small one I encountered in the Forest.

I hurried into the house to obtain a saucer of milk but when I returned bearing my creamy gift he had gone.

They move swiftly when the occasion requires it — when seen from the rear they resemble an old lady hurrying to catch a bus. A friend in a neighbouring village has a family of them which come nightly for milk with unfailing regularity.

They make friends easily and are delightful creatures who mate in an upright position snout to snout and belly to belly with many musical grunts of endearment and satisfaction. I have never seen this myself as these urchins of the night are not often encountered when they are love-making, but a friend witnessed it one summer evening when walking by a hedgerow. He heard what he took to be the murmuring of human lovers until he investigated and found them to be spiny ones.

A tortoiseshell has decided it is time to hibernate and has chosen a shrouded corner of our outdoor loo. It is a tiny specimen, half the usual size. If it survives it will enjoy a long sleep of some forty weeks. Peacocks and tortoiseshells seek winter quarters very early — often in the month of August, but mostly in September, before the hedgehogs retire for the winter.

Hedgehogs do not go into hibernation until October — some leave it too late and get caught by the first frosts. The location of the winter retreat is carefully chosen: hollow roots, rubbish and timber heaps (some perish when such heaps are burnt in late autumn), haystacks, and behind dense evergreen creepers against walls.

These amusing urchins of the night have few enemies, save foxes and badgers and marauding dogs — it is doubtful if a rat would tackle a hedgehog, and a dog is usually unable to unroll them.

On summer nights when out hunting they have a varied diet of earth worms, slugs, insects of all kinds, even pheasant and partridge eggs and young birds if they can catch them. They eat noisily and breathe heavily, snoring and grunting like old gentlemen short of wind.

August 28

I discovered a new wood today in company with the fair Elizabeth — a wood which is almost equal in size to our own Forest.

It was one of those delightful afternoons when there is a distinct feel of coming autumn. On every hand from countless fields arose clouds of fragrant smoke rising in tall pillars into the quiet sky, and the sun itself was veiled as with gauze.

We left the car by the Forester's house and walked up the track which was flanked, surprisingly, with walnut trees, some laden with nuts, and acacia trees. In a little while we reached another ride by a stand of oak. Here, for some forty yards or so from the track, the ground had been cleared of trees and shrubs. In this broad band of open ground, willow herb and thistles grew in abundance with clumps of knapweed. Here we found an amazing sight.

As far as the eye could see hundreds of butterflies were on the wing, mostly peacocks in mint condition, commas (showing that burning red orange which stands out so vividly) and painted ladies. Some of the latter were tattered and pale, others beautifully fresh, obviously hatched locally on the thistles. This has been a great summer for painted ladies, the best for some years. A few small coppers were also flying, together with common blues.

To see this great concourse of butterflies reminded me of days long gone when every wayside was a-bob with them before the invention of insecticides. It seemed that every thistle and knapweed head held a sidling peacock or painted lady, the latter contrasting in colour with the rich red tones of the peacocks. Here and there flickered the pale primrose yellow of the brimstones and the glowing brick red of the commas.

The peacocks, when at rest with wings closed, resembled the dark sails of little ships. Almost every silvery thistle had its dark peaked 'sail', though the butterflies were of course feeding on the crimson flowers amongst the fluffy seeds.

Yet despite this great array of coloured wings, there was something in the air that told me so surely of coming autumn — the misty veiled sunlight — the silver plumes on the thistles, the dark olive green of the oaks unstirred by breeze, heavy and weary looking. There was almost a smell, too, of summer's end — the scent of dried sun-baked grass mingled with the faint tang of stubble burning. Distant trees were cloaked in that faint blue haze — a glaze if you like — such as the old oil painters used on their canvases.

Less than twenty years ago the sun-baked grasses, no longer lush and green, would be shrilling with grasshoppers. They, like the frogs, have gone. The last grasshoppers I heard and saw were in the New Forest in July, then their high 'shivering' sound seemed to be the very voice of high summer.

This great forest — once the heart of Rockingham Forest in the Middle Ages — was once all oak and ash; now it is chiefly regiments of the hateful conifers which stretch to the horizon. Wild creatures do not like these dark woods where little sunlight can penetrate to the forest floor — only the wild deer prefer the shade, and those rascals of the bird world, the jay, magpie and carrion crow.

On the fringe of this forest is a place called Morehay Lawn where, in the Middle Ages, the deer found pasturage, the clearing in the trees allowing grass to grow. These spaces were termed 'lawns' — in all the ancient forests of England you will find 'lawns'. Here and there in that lonely place are still some very ancient oaks — now stag headed — which must be three or four hundred years old, their wriggly tines protruding from

148

the uninteresting level-green sea of conifers, truly like the horns of stags.

The shadows were long when Elizabeth and I retraced our steps. I was glad of trouser legs to protect me from the thistles but my fair companion was stockingless, her feet in sandals, yet she did not flinch from the briers, thistles, and rough ground — a real comely country girl with a deep love of nature, preferring the woods and fields to 'discos' and city life.

A solemn stillness seemed to rest upon the great wood and the quiet fields, that sense of pause — the growing season over and done, the waiting for the fall of the leaf and the gloomy short days, what I call the 'dark tunnel of winter', when the sun has retreated from us.

No cloud in the sky — no movement in leaf or tree, anywhere, save the flicker of a butterfly's wing and a regiment of white ducks, waddling through the grass of an orchard, where rosy apples showed and wasps were busy over the fallen fruit as the golden gauzy minutes crept away to evening.

The last purple emperor's egg hatched at ten a.m. this morning; half an hour later the tiny larvae had crept to the extremity of the leaf. Its life was short. When I looked again into the breeding cage this evening I saw it being attacked by yet another of the wretched flower-bug creatures and was too late to save my precious infant. How unfortunate it is that life can only continue by feeding on itself, from the minutest creature only visible through a microscope to man himself — what a chancy wasteful business it all is!

Now I think I have solved the difficulty of this predatory business, albeit too late for this season. Hitherto I have always had a thick 'bush' of sallow in my net cage. Now I have pruned away almost all of the bush, leaving just the four sprays of leaves on which my surviving larvae (nine) are feeding. This enables me to see clearly any predatory beetle on the leaves, top and bottom (the underside often harbours the leaf bug). Each larvae only requires a single leaf to eat and they rarely wander from it once they have taken up their position on the peak, and there they will remain until the time of hibernation.

When autumn comes and the leaves fall and wither, the larvae then seek out the stem of the sallow and usually hibernate where a twig joins the main stem. When summer comes again the larvae then require a lot of leaves and can be moved to 'spare' sallows. When they are half grown they can look after themselves, so the hibernating tree only has few branches. If I had adopted this method at egg-collecting time I should now have over a dozen larvae, possibly my full complement (fourteen eggs collected in the summer of 1980), whereas I lost five to the flower bugs.

The dreadful sunless and wet months of July and August (with but a few breaks) meant the female purple emperors would not lay. This was coupled with the fact that in May and early June there was a prolonged drought and much sun which induced an infestation of the sallows by all manner of bugs and tortrix larvae, playing havoc with all the oak trees as well as the sallows.

September 5 ———————————

When I looked into my studio this
morning to see how the swallows' second
brood was faring, I beheld a fearful scene.
The nest had fallen off the sloping wall and lay on its side on
top of a wooden cupboard below. Three young were sprawled
on the top of it and another on the floor. All were feeble and
cold, though they were well feathered.

What an appalling scene! My beloved swallows!

I could see what had happened. The growing brood filled
the nest. No doubt the parents alighted on the rim to feed.
The weight was too great, nest and babies were precipitated
into the abyss!

Quick thinking was now needed. How was I to secure the
nest to the sloping wall? Then I remembered I had a short pair
of steps in the woodshed.

I picked up the comatose babies, and put them back into
the well-feathered nest which mercifully was intact and quite
undamaged — even the warm lining was undisturbed. The
steps were fetched. These I placed on the cupboard top and
fixed the nest back against the wall with its base resting on the
top step.

Now — the question was, would the parents desert?
There was no sign of them flying round against the dull cloudy
sky which was spitting rain.

Then I noticed a strange phenomenon. There was not a
single swallow (or indeed any bird) to be seen anywhere in the
sky — nor were they visible over the village. It seemed that
they had vanished from the scene! Surely they could not have
migrated? Impossible! Earlier in the morning they were hawking everywhere. Yet, when later I went to the local market

151

town of Thrapston there was no swallow or martin to be seen there — not even hawking about the river.

This gave me hope. Maybe the dull rainy day, so gloomy after a spell of sun, had made the birds retire to barn and tree for shelter. Then, during the afternoon, the clouds rolled away and to my great joy I saw the parent swallows darting in and out of the studio once more, obviously feeding their brood which I hope were undamaged by the dreadful fall.

I have an idea that many swallows' and martins' nests fall each summer when the brood becomes large and heavy, for the nest, made of mud, is weighty. I know of two cases in the village — one where a woman rang me up with great dismay to say her martins' nest had fallen from the wall and smashed to pieces in the street. She had managed to gather up the young and had them in a basket. What could she do? I told her to put them in an open box and put the brood by her window. This she did. She later rang me to say all had safely flown.

The other nest, built high in a garage, had likewise fallen but in this case the young could fly, so all was well. It remains now to see if my studio babies can manage to survive. The time is late. Soon the parents will feel bound to obey the inexorable laws of nature — the call to be up and away. It will be a close-run thing.

A keeper friend, Jack Long, rang me up last night to ask me if I would like to try for a mallard duck, as over a hundred ducks were coming at twilight to a barley stubble on his shoot.

Stubble duck are worthy game, the season of barley harvest is short, and so I decided to go. Polar the labrador was kitted out with his camouflage coat — a most necessary process as his pale colour shows up in the dusk — and at half past seven I was up under a straggly thorn hedge which overlooked the barley stubble.

The evening was perfectly still, not a breath moved the hawthorn leaves of my ambush, gnats danced and swayed, and everywhere there was the hush and scents of autumn. Far away, a combine was at work, grumbling faintly over the rim of the field behind me. In front of me on the other side of the valley, lights began to star out from the distant town until there was a necklace of brilliant jewels all along the horizon.

So often I have seen this when wildfowling on the coast — lights seen over a great expanse of water like the Solway seem much nearer than they really are. There was that faint, warm, cosy smell in the air of cut straw stubble. Somewhere a dog was barking incessantly at a distant farm.

As the light faded and the distant lights of the town became more brilliant, wandering gnats appeared like incoming duck, and a bat even more so. This creature seemed to have a fascination for my hide, for it kept flickering to and fro in front of my face.

Then the first lot of duck appeared. They came right over me very high — a whispering bow of wings; their low, stuttering quacks seemed to be muted and secretive. They knew where they were going — it wasn't to our barley stubble but the big one just behind me.

Peering through the hedge, I saw them setting their wings and careering about the field for mallard — like wild geese — always take a 'recce' before alighting, but they were off our ground. An inexperienced gun would have fired at that bunch as they came over — there must have been close on thirty in the pack, but I held my fire.

Some smaller packs came later — one taking me unawares, closing their wings and diving overhead. I could hear the hiss of air in their wings, but I was too late. When it was nearly dark I had the only possible shot of the night at a bunch of nine which came in from my left — intent on the stubble behind us. I did not connect, and the ducks went on.

Jack the keeper had a shot or two, and so did one of our other companions who said he had a duck down in the hedge. We sent the dogs in, and Jack's spaniel wiped Polar's eye, emerging from the thicket with a mallard duck in its mouth, which the keeper very generously gave to me. These brief autumn ambushes are most enjoyable. I must confess I am very partial to stubble duck and orange sauce!

Each night when I put my dog to bed, I shine the torch into my studio and see the four young swallows in their nest on top of the steps I had placed against the wall. They huddle in a bundle for warmth, and close by sit the devoted parents perched on a string across the ceiling. To me there is something particularly touching — the little family, saved from starvation by my own hand, and the steadfast parents pressed close together nearby, keeping guard. The year is late, and many of the other swallow families in the village have departed (those in my garage certainly have — they left more than a fortnight since).

Any day now the studio brood should fly, yet what a perilous moment it must be for them — that instant when wings are spread for the first time. Maybe this brood will remember the sudden collapse of the nest and the horrid descent to the ground when their wings were still feeble and unformed.

Young birds — like humans and other animals — grow during the dark hours of sleep. This is most noticeable in young birds. I have reared many from the nest — from the time their eyes are barely open to the time of sustained flight. Always in the mornings the development was most marked, the feathers longer, the body larger.

I am anxious for my studio babies. It is dark now at eight p.m. and I am fearful that the parents will feel it is time for the long flight south. So powerful is this urge that they often forsake a late brood and leave them to starve. I have noticed lately that the parents sit during the day a little distance from the nest, facing the brood — no doubt urging them to fly and try their wings.

A farmer friend told me that this year has been a particularly good breeding season for them and he has double the usual number in his barns. Sometimes if a cat appears it is set upon by the adult birds — they dive bomb' the cats, scaring them so much that they run away.

This was a day of triumph for me and for my swallow brood. They flew soon after sun was up and arranged themselves in a bundle, close to each other, on the telephone wire outside my bedroom window.

It was as though the parents had brought their children there to exhibit them in triumph and gratitude, but of course it was nothing of the sort. This wire is close to the curved western wall of the house and is sheltered from the chill winds. It has always been a favourite 'nursery' wire for my swallows. This evening there was much anxiety and to-ing and fro-ing to get the brood safely back into the shelter and security of the studio.

In time this was accomplished. Fortunately, because the evening, though humid, was grey and full of rain. Later, after darkness had fallen, I shone my light into the room and Pa, Ma, and the kids were all close together on the ceiling string — the parents side by side at one end of the row. It had been an exciting day for them. I thought how strange it was that, had I not returned that morning to my studio, those four little bright beings would now be decaying rubbish and no doubt the bereaved parents would have departed.

So now, these perils being over, a greater peril awaits them on their long journey. I hope and pray they do not finish up in some greasy foreign belly, for the dastardly practice of netting and shooting the swallows and martins on their migration flights through the Alps still continues despite requests from more enlightened and civilized countries.

A doctor's wife in a neighbouring village told me that her house-martins, which build every year under the eaves of their house in Cranford, had reared two broods and that both had flown safely and had migrated at the end of August. When they had young it was impossible to sit on the lawn near the nest as the old birds went berserk — 'dive bombing' anybody nearby. In this the martins resembled the swallows of my farmer friend which mobbed any stray cat which ventured near.

The greatest enemy of the house-martin is the house-sparrow, which takes over the martins' nest as soon as it is completed. If martins favoured my house for building I would deal with these little pests which build such untidy nests and are given to vulgar gutter brawls. Alas! I have no overhanging eaves and my efforts to attract martins by placing artificial nests under my guttering have failed. The artificial nests have been taken over by bats.

September 20

This evening at about six p.m. after a day of almost unbearable humidity and low cloud, I looked upwards to see, at a great height above the quiet fields, a great concourse of migrating swallows.

They were so high I could barely see them, and as they flew southwards they hawked hither and thither, for swallows do not fly in a direct line like migrating geese; they feed as they fly and can thus refuel to sustain energy as they travel on their long journey.

For some reason the sight of this great army of my most loved summer visitors filled me with a great sorrow. I wondered why this should be. Was it because they epitomise for me the passing of the long summer days, with all the wealth of growth and abundant life? Was it envy, envy for their effortless passage to sunlit lands? Was it because we do not see these winged arrows again for another seven months, when days are so short and darkness comes early?

The cuckoo comes in April and we rejoice to hear him — he goes unheard, unseen. The dusky swifts arrive to take the cream of our English summer (though it must be confessed that they are terrible town lovers) and depart without a tear from me.

I suppose the reason for my melancholy is that we actually see the departure of our loved ones and know that it will be long before we welcome them again. If they slipped away like the cuckoo and the swift, the parting would be less painful.

I should have no such sentiments if I saw the wild geese departing in the spring, though the sight of the incoming migrating skeins which reach these shores each autumn fills me with wonder and delight. There is no sadness there for me. I have witnessed the arrival of the geese from the Arctic on several occasions in Scotland. Tremendously moving it is, for when they first appear, at the end of September and more generally in late October, they can be seen as mere faint specks, like seeds, in the upper atmosphere. As the skeins see their well-loved, chosen winter quarters they split up and scatter, each bird closing its wings to spill the air from them. They come tumbling earthwards like a sycamore leaf in an autumn gale, and with a joyous outcry.

Yet my little studio family has not yet departed. Tonight, to my delight, I again saw the whole family perched on the string in my studio — all clustered together for warmth. Each morning now they return to the telephone wire outside my bedroom window but soon they will be gone, following the great thronged highway of the skies.

I removed their old nest from the studio wall for it was only supported by the wooden steps I placed there. It weighed over a pound. I admired the way each little mud pellet had been cemented together to form the complete cup of the nest. It was quite clean within and free from fleas, lined with soft hen feathers and wisps of dried grass.

The hen feathers must have come from the farm in the village, or maybe further a-field. No small wonder it came adrift from the wall, for when full of well-grown young, plus the parents perching on the rim, I estimated that it must have weighed at least two pounds. I have now fastened a strip of wood just below where the nest was built so if they come next spring — which I hope and pray they will, there will be some support for the nest.

Swallows will always build high up next to the ceiling, leaving a space of some three inches between the top of the mud rim and the actual ceiling, which becomes marked just there by the brushing of their little dusty heads.

In the hedgerows now the climbing vines of the wild hop are turning saffron yellow, there are golden leaves in the chestnuts, and the limes and the fruit trees, along with the wild cherries, are the first to show the burning fires of autumn.

No longer do the stubble fires veil the weakening sun, but the oaks are still green enough. They will be the last to turn, some of them will show buff and brown up to Christmas in their lower boughs.

News comes of a hobby nesting in a forest in this side of the county. According to the keeper they reared one young one. I have never seen this lovely little falcon in Northampton-shire, though I have seen it in Wiltshire and Wales.

Wiltshire is very rich in bird and insect life. On the ranges of the downs near Westbury an astonishing number of rare birds are found — most damning evidence against the use of agricultural sprays and pesticide for these are not used on the army ranges. Alas! The stone curlew has not been seen breed-ing there for some years, though it is still seen on passage.

I knew the area around Imber so well, for as a boy I used to ramble over the downs with my brothers. In my book *A Child Alone* I described a strange secret lagoon we came upon one day after a hot ramble over the downs. It was partially dry — a great area of cracked earth but with banks of tall reeds in which we found the deserted nests of reed warblers, the broods having flown, for it was late August.

I have often thought about that lonely place and to my delight I received a letter recently from a reader of *A Child Alone*, telling me he had visited that very locality in the summer of 1980 and giving me the map reference of it.

This writer has a special permit to visit the artillery ranges in his capacity of Nature Conservancy member, and he gave me a list of the rare birds which frequent the area — the most important being the rare raptors — hen harriers, hobbies, short-eared owls and buzzards.

I wonder if the red-backed shrike is still found on the Wiltshire downs? It was comparatively common between the wars and we found several nests. It is a species which is now as rare as the corncrake and even the 'common' bunting, in the south country. The decline of the common bunting is something of a puzzle. Less than forty years ago I used to see them every year on the telephone wires to the north of Northampton, but I have not heard or seen one for a long time now. The reason for its disappearance may be the modern methods of agriculture. With the coming of the mechanical reaper, both for corn and grass, the nest — which is always built upon the ground and is most difficult to find — is exposed by the shuttling knives. The lark has suffered in the same way.

I have recently had a letter from that fine naturalist and sportsman Arthur Cadman, who once lived in the New Forest, about the red adder I saw there in July. He tells me he only saw one red one once, as a boy in Yorkshire, but never in the New Forest where the adder is common, as plentiful perhaps as it is in the highlands of Scotland.

The New Forest adders always had a grey-green or blue background to the black back pattern. This was so in the adders I saw on the old airfield at Brawdy in South Wales some years ago.

I also saw some smooth snakes there — our rarest snake and quite harmless. At first sight it might be mistaken for an adder as it has a dim blurred pattern down the back, but it is a more slender serpent with a neater head than either adder or grass snake. Some people have a horror of even the harmless grass snake, yet I find them beautiful creatures — not in the least sinister, though it must be admitted that this only applies to our British snakes — some of the pit vipers and puff adders are distinctly awesome.

A great friend, Valezina, Viscountess Bolingbroke, presented me with a beautiful water-colour sketch of a grass snake drawn by her father — the celebrated F. W. Frohawk who wrote and illustrated the classic volumes of *British Butter-flies*, now scarce collectors' items. I suppose Frohawk knew more about our British butterflies than anyone in the present century. His drawings of each butterfly on the British list, with its food plant, larva, and chrysalis, are exquisite works of art. It was Frohawk who discovered the secret of the large blue in Britain — a species which is now thought to be extinct but which I am certain must still occur in some undiscovered locality in North Devon or Gloucestershire.

The late John Moore, who was also a great friend of mine (we did several talks for the BBC together), told me of a Gloucestershire locality, but I do not intend to divulge its map reference, for the large blue may still fly in that area.

I am reminded of the story of a doctor friend (who was a keen collector), of how, when he was motoring in Devon, he stopped his car in a lonely lane and climbed over a field gate to spend a penny. He found himself in a colony of large blues. The strange thing is that he was never able to find the place again and was unable to pinpoint the exact spot.

The last recognised locality for the large blue in Gloucestershire was ploughed up during the last war, and the rough hillsides with the food plant, wild thyme, and its ant hills, which are necessary to the life cycle of Arion, have gone forever.

It was on June 3, 1905, that Frohawk opened up an ants' nest in North Devon and found the full-grown larvae of the large blue, thus solving a mystery which had been a puzzle to entomologists for many years — what happened to the young larva after it fed on the wild thyme. The ants take them down to their nests where they are looked after and 'milked' until ready to pupate, which they do in the darkness of the ants' nest — feeding, strange to say, on the ants' larvae, and actually hibernating in the nest all winter to emerge as butterflies the following June.

Frohawk's description of the whole process is as fascinating as anything Maeterlinck wrote about the honey bee. Frohawk, one of the most famous naturalists of our day, never had any true recognition beyond becoming a Fellow of the Royal Entomological Society and an M.B.O.U.

September 22

After a night of pealing thunder and torrential rain, the forest was damp and steaming as I made my way up the narrow path between the brambles. Only the *triste* song of a robin broke the stillness.

In the soft ground was the neat cloven spoor of the fallow deer. A few tortoiseshells and peacocks were busy over the knapweed flowers and blackberry blossom. There was the sweet damp smell of the oaks everywhere.

From deep in the thickets on the right of the main ride came the strange medieval sound of a rutting fallow buck — a coughing grunt oft repeated, a sound which must have echoed in this great Forest of Rockingham from Roman times.

The meadowsweet flowers are over. Only the seeded heads remain, and I saw a brood of young bullfinches, with their attendant parents, busy gathering the ripe brown crumbling seeds. As I approached they dipped away into the thickets, showing the white rumps which contrast so well with their blue-black tails.

They put me in mind of a strange little story. Some years ago I reared a bullfinch from the nest, before it was fully fledged. To my great joy, when October came and it began to shed its flank feathers, I saw sheaves of bright pink which showed it was a cock bird. Even when it was barely out of the nest I taught it a tune, for bullfinches will learn quite complicated airs. The bird fanciers of the Black Forest teach their bullies quite lengthy tunes.

For a number of years this little cock was my constant companion. On summer days I placed him on a table in the garden so he could enjoy the sunlight and open air. I would never keep a trapped wild bird in a cage, which is a wicked thing to do, but a bird reared almost from the egg, which has always

162

known you as a parent, is perfectly happy in a roomy cage with plentiful natural food.

One afternoon in summer my pet was out on the lawn for his usual airing when a great gust of wind arose. The cage fell off the table with a crash, the door flew open, and when I rushed out there was no sign of my little cock — he had flown away. The sudden shock of the fall, the crash of the cage, must have been a fearful experience.

The summer passed to autumn. Then one day — walking up to the forest — I suddenly heard the familiar piped tune coming from the hedge and there was my dear little pal. He had seen and recognised me and immediately piped his tune! I plucked some meadow-sweet seed and called him Without a pause he flew straight to my hand and I took him home. He seemed delighted to be back in his old haunts after his jaunt in the wild.

Then one day, after I had given him a bath, I inadvertently left the cage door ajar. When I returned the cage was empty and my little pal had gone — this time for good. I never saw him again. No doubt he preferred the life of the wild, and I was glad for him, though whether he survived the following hard and bitter winter I do not know. Perhaps the brood I saw feeding on the meadowsweet were descendants of my little cock. I liked to think they were.

A little way up this ride, my retriever Polar dived into the brambles and put up a woodcock which flew across my front and dropped into the underwood. This would be one of the resident breeding woodcock and not an emigrant, for the latter do not arrive with us until the October moon — the Hunter's Moon. These solitary 'loners' are strange little birds who live out their secret lives in the damp woodlands, resting in the day-time in thick cover and feeding at night in the ditches and dykes.

How different from the other gregarious hen-footed fowl — the waders, and the goose and duck tribes who are never happy unless in the company of others. The snipe, though occasionally a solitary feeder, is often found in 'whisps', and the plover family also is gregarious, though the grey plover sometimes feeds alone. I can think of no other bird on the British list which chooses the hermit's life, most have their mates with them for company.

As a sporting bird, the woodcock is grossly overrated — a plover or moorhen on the table is vastly superior — nor is it difficult to shoot unless in very thick cover. Its habit of carrying its young between its thighs when disturbed at the nest has long been a subject of contradiction and debate. Many sportsmen in 'woodcock country' have never witnessed this, yet I have first-hand evidence of a woodcock which not only carried off one of its young from the nest site but returned repeatedly to pick up the rest of the brood, transferring them to a safer place. A naturalist friend was lucky enough to witness this when walking in the woods, and I once saw a moorhen fly away from its nest with a young bird between its thighs, though it dropped the chick in transit across the meadow.

The delicate pencilling and rich ambers and browns of the woodcock's plumage is of great beauty, echoing all the subtle colours of fallen oak leaves and the ashen tints of dead and bleached holly leaves (the woodcock loves to spend the daylight hours under holly bushes). It is a stout and sturdy little person and the large expressive dark eye is sometimes the only feature which betrays the hiding bird as it crouches in the withered bracken and fallen leaves.

October 2 _____

One remaining swallow — possibly
the youngest of the second brood
— still returns each night to roost on
the electric cable in my studio. The
parents and their other three young left a week ago when there
was a puff of north wind to help them on their way.

Today, on an afternoon of gentle low sun and yellowing
chestnut leaves, I came upon a strange and poignant place in
my rambles. A ruined cottage, the blackened ribs of the once-
thatched roof still visible, a weed-grown garden, some forty
yards by twenty, close to a narrow lane — a few decaying fruit
trees and a rusting pallisade of horse-radish rods down in
one corner.

I entered what was once the garden by a broken-down
gate which hung at an angle on its hinges, still retaining traces
of pale blue paint. The afternoon held that solemn silence of
autumn, and the only sound was that of a robin singing in a
damson tree which was leaning wearily close to the
ruined house.

The garden was a veritable jungle of weeds — dock, with
its hooked burrs; the huge limp elephantine leaves of rhubarb,
now turning saffron yellow; thistles whose silver plumes were
poised for take-off at the next puff of wind. Tall nettles — the
mean, lofty species which will give a sting which will last for a
week — grew along the hedge where elderberries, in black and
shining clusters, drooped low with their luscious weight — a
future feast for starlings newly in from overseas.

There was a leaning apple tree also, propped up by a stout
fork of ash. I could visualize the long-dead inhabitant of this
cottage propping up the leaning tree, possibly after an
equinoctial storm when it was heavily laden with fruit. A few

165

brilliant scarlet apples showed among the upper boughs, and some lay among the nettles where wasps were busy transforming them into hollow shells, helped no doubt by field voles. Close to the vacant doorless opening to the house was a clump of Michaelmas daisies, meagre flowers of an anaemic pink. Upon them I counted seventeen tortoiseshell butterflies, sidling and sipping the sweet nectar. Every insect was of identical shape, pattern and colouring as though turned out by a printing machine, a pattern unchanged through a million years.

What is it that fascinates me about the colouring of the tortoiseshell? Perhaps it is a memory of childhood days when butterflies were not insects but elusive, desirable, delicate jewels. the flowing orange red contrasting with the black bars on the forewings reminded me of a burning fire behind the bars of a gate and, wonder of wonders! if you look closer there are specks of heavenly blue peeping in the black mosaic of the wing edges like darts in a Persian carpet. In the pale October sun they flitted daintily from flower to flower, wings wide-spread to get the full benefit of the last low rays of the sun.

I peered into the empty shell of the cottage, at the blackened hearth. What and when was the last meal cooked there? Who lived and died in this humble cottage after years of toil in the fields — winter and summer, spring and autumn? No doubt, on many a golden afternoon such as this, the aproned lady of the house sat by the door peeling apples or potatoes whilst the tortoiseshells played about the flowers. The place reminded me of an old tumbledown birds' nest in a winter hedge, all awry and filled with mouse-gathered berries.

The garden would have been well tended some fifty years ago — no docks or nettles, but neat rows of peas and beans, and potatoes nicely ridged. It had obviously been a farm labourer's cottage, for half a mile on, up the side of a southern-facing hill, was a gaunt pale stone farmhouse and a high wall like a desert fort.

I stood listening to the sad little song of the robin and watched the setting sun twinkle and glow as it sank behind the thinning elder bushes which were already losing some of their rose pink leaves. The wild bryony in the hedge, with its spade-shaped leaves, was dying too — the leaves a pale saffron yellow. There was the very faint smell of burning weeds in the still air — it was goodbye to summer, the robin was singing farewell.

Only a week ago I saw a pair of them locked in vicious combat on my lawn. They were fighting like little demons, and I believe I could have picked them up, they were so enraged. The truth is that robins are pugnacious birds, quite belying their apparently friendly natures. They have strong territorial rights and these are staked out at autumn time and defended with vigour.

As I stood in that deserted garden with nettles and docks almost to my waist, I watched the evening gnats dancing — their minute wings gauzy in the dying rays of the sun. Over the gaunt black spikes of the roof timbers the sky was gold, suffused with pink, and a little band of twittering swallows passed across sinking from side to side as they flew. I fancied they were on migration as they were heading southwards, but then they turned and flew aimlessly back towards the farm on the hill, young birds no doubt, like my lone baby at home, not yet strong enough to go.

The glitter in the elder tangle faded. High to the west one single golden wisp cloud marked the setting of the sun.

October 4 _____

I looked into my dusky studio at last light. *There was no swallow roosting on the electric light cable*! It had gone at last on its long journey.

I felt a strange pang when I saw the vacant wire, for I knew all the long dark days of winter must pass before scything blue wings sweep up once more into the studio for I shall surely keep the door open from mid April onwards. It left not a day too soon, for now the grey wind blows — the tall spires of the

Lombardy poplars are leaning and threshing, though their leaves are still green, defying decay.

There is a chill in the wind. I passed a stubble field in the late afternoon where a tractor was working in an oncoming storm of rain. Dark storm clouds made it seem like evening, and one solitary black rook winged its weary way across the buff-coloured field. I could paint that scene, I think. It was so typical of autumn, with that single black bird oaring its lonely way towards the distant sunset, the drab buff of the field, the dark ragged hedge, the distant black tractor lurching across the stubble leaving in its wake the dark fresh-turned earth glistening in the soft, falling rain.

Lucky little swallow! Sun-worshipper, bringer of hope and of life everlasting.

A recent visit to Welney Washes was rewarding. There the sun shone pale and without warmth but the far end of the lagoon opposite the viewing room was alive with wigeon and mallard.

The latter were going absolutely mad, hurling themselves into the glittering water, diving and re-appearing in flurries of foam through the sheer joy of life — exulting in their hour of sun and health. It was real 'horse' (or should I say 'duck') play, for they were larking about with one another — the wigeon also.

I prefer Welney Washes to other reserves I have seen because all the fowl you see are truly wild and unpinioned. Four Berwick swans were on the far grass — the main swan flock had not yet arrived. One or two ruff were on the grass and two pairs of aloof shovellers, tubby and smug, rode the blue ripples of the lagoon in the low rays of the afternoon sun.

Last time I was at Welney it was mid-winter and the low-lying 'washes' had gone under and were sheeted in ice. The frozen lagoon before the viewing room was locked fast in ice. Upon it lumbered the unwieldy swans to spike some swedes which lay upon the frozen surface. They skidded and slipped all over the place and one swan, coming in to land, slid for fifteen yards, knocking over some tubby wigeon which were too late in getting out of the way.

The winter sky was full of serried skeins and teams of duck — an unforgettable sight. So it must have been before the draining of the fens.

On our way home I topped the flood bank of the '100 foot' and saw below me the white-sheeted figure of a fowler crouched in the tall, rusting reeds. He had a liver and white spaniel beside him and clutched his 12-bore in mittened hands. He wore a balaclava helmet and his nose was as red as a carrot. It might have been a scene from Colonel Hawker's day — the fowler in ambush clad in his white sheet amidst the tall plumed reeds — the grey leaden sky, the white frozen plain, which stretched to the horizon broken only by the half-submerged bushes along a dyke and field gates standing nakedly in the flood and the odd fence which marked the boundary of the washes.

October 24 _____

Almost overnight the wayside trees — the oaks and ashes — have turned a rich contrast of reds, browns, ambers, a warm ochre. The garden pond (Big Pond) has been transformed into an Indian carpet — a rich mosaic of colour from the black poplars, birch, and beech.

In a recent golden afternoon a distinguished visitor arrived bobbing his autumn-tinted breast on a slender sweeping branch of a willow overhanging the water. Big-headed, big-billed, his tiny carmine feet clutching the slender bough — a kingfisher! his plumage more suited to a steamy jungle. He scrutinised the water below, dived head-first in and emerged with an infant roach which he took up to the old stone sun dial where he belaboured it into insensibility. He then turned it round in a deft movement and gulped it down.

Kingfishers have the sharpest sight of any bird — they need to, for a fish below the surface of the water can be no easy target. They have to allow for refraction. He saw me at the french window and departed over the apple trees — a line of vivid incandescent blue. He (I judged it to be a male but the sexes are dressed alike) comes from time to time from the stream down in the village in the banks of which they breed each summer.

I have an idea that, like the fork-tailed kite, they are on the increase. When I was walking across the water meadows near Oundle tonight, hoping to ambush a mallard on the flood water, one came past my head with the swiftness of a humming bird. The average person would not have seen it, or if they had would not have recognised it as a kingfisher. A brisk wind which has been blowing all day was still stirring in the willows, but as evening advanced it died away.

I stood in the shadow of some ancient hawthorns whose roots are awash most winters, for these flat meadows flood rapidly after a day of rain. The clouds I hoped would stay dissolved away, and the sun went down with scarce a wisp of gold in the west. The willows, as yet still green, became dark against the afterglow, but alas! these spacious meadows are no longer the 'quiet fields' which once they were. From time to time, thundering low-flying jets passed over, gouts of smoke and flames spewing from their posteriors — a hideous racket which must be terrifying for the wildfowl which haunt these riverside pastures.

We seem to have become so used to noise just as people can get used to obnoxious smells if they live in the vicinity of hound kennels, glue factories, brick and iron works, and piggeries. Thirty years ago there would have been no sound of traffic or low-flying planes here, only the wailing of peewits and the distant cries of children at play.

To the east, a huge golden globe of light appeared slyly over the distant trees. For a moment I wondered what it was, for it seemed twice the size of a normal full moon. Soon it had hoisted itself clear of the trees as the earth rolled onwards and became reflected in the strip of flood water which shone like a pale spear in the centre of the field, a majestic double vision. A single mallard drake, quacking loudly, flew against the fast-dimming sunset, but he did not come my way, wise fowl.

171

The sun gone, the moon took over with its ghostly light, throwing a feeble shadow from me as I tramped back to the car — duckless, but glad to have felt and seen the coming of night and the Hunter's moon, for this was indeed the Hunter's moon, and I was the hunter, returning empty-handed but content.

I have replaced the glass pane in my garage door, for the swallows have long gone and I give no hospitality to house-sparrows. In any case they are well able to look after themselves. Their favourite dormitory is under the pantiles of the garage roof — a small crack which would seem to be too narrow to admit the entry of a plump sparrow.

In the mornings, if the sun shines, they gather there to gossip as in a market place, and warm themselves; it is a rendezvous for starlings too. Sheltered from the north wind the old tiles are warm to their feet and little bellies. Now and again a sparrow will squeeze into the hole. The starlings also seem fascinated by it, though they cannot squeeze in. They chatter and gibber and peer into the dark slit, turning their heads on one side to see what is within like inquisitive parrots.

These curved tiles are not made these days — they are far too heavy and cumbersome and need stout timber to sustain their weight. They are commonly found in Norfolk and in some of the villages and towns in the fens, but are not now so common in Northamptonshire.

In springtime when the starlings hunt for nesting sites they make strenuous efforts to squeeze into the 'sparrows' house'. Once one became stuck and I saw its legs threshing frantically as it tried to free itself. Now winter is almost here this particular roof ridge forms a concert platform for these spangled vulgar members of the bird world. In the winter sun they stretch wide their bills and open their wings which they waggle in ecstasy.

In their winter plumage of stars and spangles they are quite beautiful; the sun plays upon their burnished feathers revealing beautiful glints of purple, green and blue. Like the wings of the male purple emperor butterfly, their colours only show in certain lights and at certain angles. Even the dignified rooks stalking the furrow show these hidden jewelled lights, the magpie also but not, I think, the jackdaw. The latter bird, more than the rook, is always found in the vicinity of stately homes, castles, and churches.

In medieval times they were regarded as the reincarnation of clerics and monks. No extensive parkland is without its jackdaws — they are the pale-eyed buglers of kings, dukes, earls, and the landed gentry. Every hollow parkland tree has its tenant, every turret and tower its familiar spirit. They delight in their aerial manoeuvres about their territories. It must be remembered that in the case of ancient castles and parks the jackdaws one sees are the descendants of others, going back to the time when the castle or mansion was first built. I remember once walking in the ruined aisles of Rivaux Abbey one autumn day and watching the jackdaws so busy about the stone arches, peering down with their pale eyes at me.

They also act as the buglers to the flocks of rooks. When the latter perform their nightly 'trooping of the colour' at edge of dark before retiring to their roosting woods the jackdaws tag behind in a noisy 'chacking' concourse, their higher call notes contrasting with the continuous excited cawing of the rooks. At edge of dusk at a certain loch in Scotland I have many times witnessed this nightly ceremony. The noise made by the rooks and attendant daws sounds like the roar of a distant waterfall.

In the darkling sky hundreds of black specks wheel and soar. These, as at a given signal, all sweep down into the hanging woods above that lovely loch. Though the rooks and daws are silenced in sleep, the quiet of the night is then broken by the hoarse croaks and cries of the greylag geese, for this is a favourite roost.

As the rooks play above the woods, the geese come winging in from the surrounding hills, and the night is full of their wild cries. During the day, they have been feeding some miles distant on some favourite pasture, but as the sun sinks they wing their way to the security of the loch. As each party arrives there is a greeting from those already there and the clamour drowns the sound of the rooks and daws.

On the shores of the loch, surrounded by beechen woods in which red squirrels abound, is the Laird's 'Big Hoose'. He used to let us have a shot sometimes at the geese when they were feeding on his estate but (alas!) he died. The estate, loch, and house was bought by a Sassenach property developer from England. So those good days are over when we ambushed the greylags in the pale cold dawn when they came to feed on the barley stubble.

The eggs of the jackdaw are quite beautiful and vary enormously in colouring. Some have a pale azure background with handsome smears of sienna grey and black, others are merely speckled with black like those of the song-thrush. To a bird-nesting boy the raiding of a jackdaw's nest had something most satisfying about it.

There was the climb up the rough barked elm and the reaching in to the mass of sticks, the soft cup of sheep's wool on which the warm smooth eggs rested. We prized the more richly marked eggs as we did the polished, rich, red-brown conkers in October time. I doubt whether there are bird-nesting boys now — it was the chief delight of the country boy half a century ago. Birds are more scarce now, so I suppose it is better that way.

November 2 _____

The sudden arrival of true winter
has taken me unawares. It seems
only yesterday that the sun shone
with warmth enough to tempt a late
tortoiseshell to the fading Michaelmas
daisies. This evening as I write this I see a frosty saffron sky —
bare poplars dipping before an arctic east wind, leaves carpet-
ing the garden and pools, almost disguising the water, and
hastening starling flocks passing across the sky, bound for
some distant roost.

Sensing the nearness of winter, the rats have come in from
their summer sojourn in the quiet fields and hedgerows — like
Caesar, they move into their winter quarters, which means
under the dog house. Twice nightly I have caught rats as big as
half-grown rabbits, and there are others — wary now of the
cunningly set 'Fenn' trap laid in the well-beaten run.

Today I inspected the five surviving larvae of my purple
emperors, each one has selected a leaf for hibernation. This is
tiresome of them — they should have gone to the main stem. If
I had left them on the dead curled leaf the coming frosts would
have dislodged the frail dead stalks, and leaf and larvae would
have fallen to the base of the net cage.

So I have bound each leaf stalk tightly to the twig and they
should be safe from all the winds that blow. This being done I
was invited by the nice lad Paul in the village to inspect his
eagle owls.

In a barn behind the village 'boozer' these two magnificent creatures sat upon their perches close to the wire,
hissing gently like kettles when I peered close. This meant they
were in truculent mood. Even though these two birds had been
reared this spring they were enormous, fully feathered, and

175

roughly as big as well-grown eaglets, and would grow larger yet. Their great golden eyes, like rising harvest moons, magnified by mist, stared into mine five inches away — only the wire separated us. In the centre of each glowing globe of orange fire the black iris, as black as a 'black hole' in space, had an almost hypnotic effect.

Occasionally an eye-lashed blind descended, hiding for an instant that glowing fire — a roughish conspiratorial wink if you like. The massive talons, like hooked six-inch nails, clasped the rough wooden perch, talons which could bind like meat hooks on to hare, small deer, or hapless osprey, for in their remote cold barrens, haunt of wolves and bear, osprey often fall victim to this largest of all living owls.

The male, as in all the birds of prey, was smaller and more brightly striated but no less fierce — indeed Paul assured me that he was the most savage of the two. With what dignity they sat there on their perches, how those four vivid orbs glowed like live coals in the gloom of the big barn!

There were other inhabitants in adjoining barns — a pair of snowy barn owls (feminine by comparison), who slyly popped in and out of their box and sailed about on silent wings, a pair of kestrels also, and, hopping about the yard, a young carrion crow with an injured wing, absurdly tame — the wisest of all Paul's guests and, so he said, the most mischievous.

But it was the great eagle owls which drew me back, again and again — their splendid ear tufts, worn like jaunty arched feathers in a medieval nobleman's cap, and the expression in those eyes which said 'if you were a sparrow I would pick your bones clean!' What truly magnificent creatures! At night they salute the hamlet with that deep booming 'ho-horoo' sound, which must echo on many a frozen night in manless icy wildernesses, a sound which must strike a sudden chill of terror to the arctic hare crouching in the snow.

The female, I noticed, suddenly switched her glowing eyes to inspect the carrion crow which was hopping about the yard playing with a bread crust, obviously a much more interesting thing to watch than a mere man!

176

The beautiful medley of greys, ambers, deep browns and purplish black in the plumage, infinitely beautiful with the most delicate bars and pencilling, gives a sense of great richness. Only the brush of Thorburn could do it full justice — indeed he has a fine study of the eagle owl in his big red volume of British Birds. Some fortunate person must have the original of that painting, which must be worth little short of a new Rolls.

What fascinated me about the owls is that it is one of the few birds whose eyes, like ours, are facing forwards and not at the side of the head as in most birds. This gives them an almost unbirdlike goblin appearance. There is no kindliness in those eyes like there is in the eyes of an old parrot or mallard; they can never take on a softness, even when they are caressing each other which this pair sometimes does.

My own little bullfinches, reared from the nest, gave me quite a friendly smile. This was especially so in my dearest little 'hen wife' my bully hen, who used to gaze into my eyes with a soft brown sweetness, she who showed the greatest delight if I had been absent for long, and offered herself to me when she sensed the spring.

Well — there it is — winter is here. In seven days' time I hope to travel north to the land of the wild geese. Like any Indian hunter I feel the tug, but there will be no horrid massacre, just a few safe well-chosen birds for the larder and I shall be content. The last relics of hunting for winter meat still stirs in some males — it is not an instinct to be ashamed of.

Standing on the lawn this early evening — watching the last sad yellow leaves of the birches drift down into the dark sepia brown of the pond, I had that sudden surge of excitement that winter is here once again — maybe it was an almost animal awareness hard to explain. We have become so used to all the so-called comforts of civilization — heated rooms, crowded cities, the hideous noise and rush and bustle of modern days, that this primitive 'outdoor' feeling, sudden and swiftly

177

passing can only be felt by your true countryman — your sportsman — naturalist.

I am sure that fine writer T. H. White had this perception — Abel Chapman too, Charles St. John, and those equally fine characters Terence Horsley, Hesketh Prichard, Millais the painter, and Selous the big-game hunter. Certainly Richard Jefferies felt it and Hudson also who was less of a dreamer than Jefferies, but with the same keen perception and with more literary skill. All these men at one period in their lives enjoyed shooting as well as studying nature, and all could write about their experiences. W. H. Hudson was a keen sportsman as a youth but later he became more 'adult' and lost the desire to 'hunt for the pot', as did Jefferies.

There is a deal of difference between your rich stock-broker or 'property developer', who slaughters tame pheasants or grouse for a few days each year, and the true hunter such as the wildfowler, who hunts alone in the wild places and cares not if he returns with an empty bag. His chief delight is in his surroundings — the magic of a winter dawn or the mystery of flighting time when, as the lights drain away, only the secret whisper of passing wings tells of wildfowl setting out for the night's foraging. At those times your 'townee sportsman' is a-bed, or indoors with artificial light and heat.

November 4

To reinforce the fact that winter is here, my garden ponds are sheeted with ice — ice which locks the fallen leaves, imbedding them as if in glass. The big golden orfe — which inhabits the middle pond and is certainly in the region of twenty years old, has retired from view, as have his two goldfish pals. They will not show again until the spring, or when the weather turns suddenly mild. They do not feed much in winter, unlike other fish, such as pike and greyling.

He had a companion, equally old, who was slain by a rogue heron which came one moonlight night in later summer.

178

It proved too large to swallow and was left on the lawn with a stab mark through its side.

Once a heron takes to raiding garden ponds it will work a district systematically, even venturing into suburban gardens. They are mostly young birds — the old ones have learnt wisdom and are very shy of humans. Their sight rivals that of the kingfisher. All the fish-eating birds have wonderful eyesight.

The osprey is in this category. I was most interested to see how an osprey breaks a dead branch for its nest. It will not, as a rule, hunt for fallen sticks, but will select a dead branch which is not too stout. He then stoops at it as though it was a fish, takes 'a run at it', the talons sweep forward, the twig is clutched and broken on impact and the bird flies on, hardly checked in flight. The long swoop which is swift and purposeful must enable the bird to hit the branch with considerable force.

With us, in the Midlands, ospreys pass through on passage, haunting waters such as Rutland and Pitsford reservoirs and even visiting large private lakes. They do not stay more than a day or so, sometimes it is an overnight stop. One of the few encouraging facts is that this noble fish-eater is apparently increasing in the Highlands of Scotland and is even colonising some of the northern tarns. 1950 was an excellent breeding year.

One eyrie I have visited is in most romantic surroundings. It is a little-known one which is visited each year — no doubt by descendants from the original eyrie at Loch an Eilean. The nest is in a pine tree on an island — a favourite locality for the osprey, and mountains close it round. In winter when the birds have migrated, the wild geese use the loch as a roosting place. In the winter dusk (as at that other Highland loch) it is a wonderful sight to see the skeins coming in from the surrounding fields. One can hear them coming long before the orderly lines appear over the snow-clad hills — the glad wild chorus which intensifies as they near their roost.

When high over the loch, they spill the air from their broad wings and descend as if by an invisible staircase, rocking from side to side. At the last moment, when some twenty feet from the surface of the loch, they set their wings, and in a graceful sweep and with down-dropped paddles, they come to rest on the water. Once down, the babel of music increases to a crescendo, heads are lowered as they gabble to each other as farmyard geese do.

I heard only recently of a so-called 'sportsman' who boasted of killing ninety-nine geese on a recent foray in Scotland. It is these unrestricted massacres which give 'wild-fowlers' a bad name. In the winter of 1979 over four hundred greylags were shot in a single day on a certain estate known to me, when the owner, who was only interested in pheasants, organised this revolting butchery.

Wild geese, if unmolested, can certainly do considerable damage to farmers' crops but their numbers can be kept in check by systematic shooting carried out by responsible people and under supervision by keepers. On this estate — well known to me — I used to see the flocks of greylags feeding contentedly in the parkland close to the 'big hoose'. I never see them now.

Wild geese cannot be displayed for sale in poulterer's shops by law, so what happened to that ghastly mound of dead geese I do not know. Such things shock our American sportsmen friends, who have strict limits on the numbers shot each season in the United States.

On one estate I know where wild geese are abundant, the number of guns is limited. One has to pay a fat fee for a morning and evening flight, nor are repeating guns allowed, and the keepers see the rules are strictly adhered to. This is as it should be.

The shooting of wild geese inland can never compare to wildfowling on the coastal marshes. In fact I have termed this 'tamefowling', though nowadays — with the estuaries and marshes grossly overshot by the 'marsh cowboys' I myself shoot geese inland, but am always careful to restrict the bag.

There have been times when, having shot my quota of five or six birds, I have put the gun down and used a camera instead.

180

Why do dogs bay at the moon? A vet may be able to advance a theory, but it is an annoying habit and is unfortunately one in which my labrador Polar seems to delight. I cannot break him of it. Hounds of course sing in kennel at the full moon and I can only think it is a relic of their wolf ancestors, but why should they bay at the moon?

My labrador Polar is not as bad as my old black Mick, who sometimes made a blood-curdling noise at dead of night. No amount of chastisement will cure them, it seems as if the pallid light has some baleful influence on them, arousing long forgotten instincts and memories. Sometimes it is sexual and there is a bitch in the vicinity, or even far off, as dogs can wind a bitch in season from over a mile or more. I had to get up twice the other night and have words with Polar. I do not like being roused in the early hours of a bitter winter's night by such melancholy music. Polar's version is more of a moan but old Mick used to sit back on his haunches like any wild wolf of Alaska and, with muzzle upraised and open wide, he really let go the most hair-raising howls.

I would be interested to know if this habit can be cured, it is quite different from the annoying barking and whining of a dog which objects to being in kennel and wishes to rejoin his master. Then chastisement is effective, as Jack Chudley the dog trainer once told me, and this is a habit which must be stamped upon at once when the dog is young.

I do not think all dogs do it; I am inclined to think it is only those which are highly strung and of nervous disposition.

The mournful baying of wolves, heard in the frozen moonlit wastes of the arctic barrenlands, is a terrible sound, as impressive perhaps as the deep-throated roar of a hunting lion. Contrary to popular belief, wolves have never been known to attack man unless infected with rabies. They have come to regard him as a very different animal comparable to a caribou, able to slay and maim from a distance, so they give us a wide berth.

Wolves in captivity may be different, even when at large, as they are at Whipsnade. It is true that in Russia they were reputed to follow a sleigh, but animals, and birds also, do not seem to connect humans with vehicles — the wolves were probably after the horses.

It just so happens that I have recently been reading an account of an incident in the Desert War. A convoy of jeeps was crossing a bare and arid plain when they saw on the horizon a herd of gazelle. It seemed a good opportunity to replenish the larder and hopes rose when the whole herd veered in their direction and actually joined the convoy. The normally shy animals came bounding alongside the jeeps keeping up with them and not a single soldier could bring himself to pull a trigger! The gazelles obviously thought the jeeps were some sort of migrating herd and so decided to join them.

One can sometimes approach within range of wild geese if one is in a landrover or car, and the animals at Longleat only vaguely seem to connect humans with cars. That is why we were able to get within a few feet of a cock capercailzie in Perthshire last winter when he stood on the road margin almost within touching distance, though it must be said that an old caper, in the breeding season, has no compunction in attacking a man.

The same lack of fear on the part of animals and birds is demonstrated by a rider on horseback who can get close to wild creatures, as I well remember from the days when I did a lot of horse riding. Partridges, and pheasants also, allow a close approach, though I think a fox, having had experience of the hunt, will make himself scarce if he sees a man on a horse.

November 16 ————————————————————————

I had a letter today from a friend of mine, an ex-policeman, now retired, who lives at Burgh le Marsh in Lincolnshire. He migrated there from the Midlands and now devotes much of his time to fishing and searching for buried treasure with one

of the new metal detectors which are so much in demand. With this he combs the beaches after storms and has assured me that he has had most satisfactory hauls of coins and other valuables.

What interested me most was his account of an uncanny experience he had when tending his cod lines far out on the desolate flats opposite his house.

His method of catching the cod is as follows. He has a long length of washing line with pegs at each end and to this is fixed short lengths of traces, each with a hook on to which is threaded the bait (lug worms) which he digs from the sands at low tide. There is a marker buoy attached to the line. When the tide has receded, the baited lines are laid out on the sand and covered up to prevent the gulls eating the lug worms.

When the tide returns these baited hooks are many feet under the surface; when it again recedes he goes out to collect the fish. Very rarely does he come home empty handed. This hobby of his is no picnic, for he has to 'work the tides' — that is to say he has to rise sometimes in the middle of the night or early morning to retrieve his catch.

Anyone who knows those desolate flats around the Wash will know that they are somewhat sinister places even in daylight and one can easily lose direction should a fog come down. The creeks, which appear of no account when the tide is out, fill and spill over and some of them can drown a man.

One moonlight night when he was far out attending his lines, he was aware of the figure of a man, apparently a wildfowler, passing by at some thirty yards distant. He had a pack of some sort on his back and what appeared to be a gun, and at his heels trotted a little dog. There was something odd about this figure, and moreover the man was apparently *walking out towards the incoming tide.*

My friend had with him a powerful torch which threw a beam like a searchlight. When he shone it on the figure the light seemed to go through it, but when he switched it off the figure again appeared, receding into the distance!

He was so intrigued he walked over to where he had first seen the ghostly fowler and examined the soft sand. There was no trace of footmarks from man or dog! Subsequent enquiries led to the story of a wildfowler and his dog who were lost, presumed drowned, on that part of the coast some years before.

My policeman friend is a very down-to-earth person, hardly the type to imagine things. I am waiting for more reports on the ghostly fowler of Burgh le Marsh!

I know the marshes of the Wash very well, as years ago I did a lot of wildfowling there, though on the south side. I too have been far out on the sands during the hours of darkness and often felt a great sense of insecurity. I always kept a keen eye on the creeks and gullies and as soon as the small pale clots of foam began to slide landwards I made tracks for the shore.

Distances can be deceptive. Shoreward lights seem close but as you walk towards the sea wall they grow no nearer. Fog is something to watch for, too, and unless you have a compass you can soon get into grave danger. Yet despite my friend's eerie experiences on the desolate flats he considers his hobby well worthwhile. He never lacks for fresh fish, and some of the cod he catches weigh as much as eight pounds.

I have done very little sea fishing (incidentally I do not think I have ever seen a beach angler hook a fish!). Years ago I went out with a boatman near St. David's Head in South Wales and caught a bag full of codling and mackerel and then hooked some leviathan which broke my stout line. What it could have been I have no idea, but my boatman got very excited and said it may have been a very large cod. My tackle was extremely strong but it parted like cotton.

November 21 _____

Of all the great tribe of anglers the pike fisherman is the most hardy. He has a certain disdainful scorn for the elements. It can freeze, it can blow, it can rain, it can snow, it makes no matter. He is to the salmon and trout fisher what the wildfowler is to the 'snoot' shooters of grouse and pheasant. He, is moreover, a solitary, a loner, he has no love of fishing matches.

I came upon such a one the other day, sitting under his green umbrella by Oundle bridge. A wicked north-east wind was blowing, sending the grey ripples chasing, and though the river itself was as yet unfrozen, the backwaters and flood flashes were thick in ice.

He had of course his green umbrella, almost as cosy as an igloo, and strewn about him were the tools of his trade, spare rods, bait box, landing net (of large dimensions), a thermos flask, sandwich box and keep nets. He was not, I sensed, very welcoming. Small blame to him. The wildfowler, crouched in his reed ambush, does not welcome strangers (or even friends). He sits like a worshipper of Buddha staring with a certain reverence at his big round float as it rides the winter wave.

My hackneyed enquiry 'any luck?' was answered with a grunt and an expectoration. So with fellow feeling I passed on, soon to disturb a snipe grubbing a ditch in the next meadow.

Let me say at once that I admire such a man. He had burning within him the very primitive instinct of the true hunter. That does not mean he will eat his pike if he catches one — in any case, pike are not good on the table unless methodically boned and disguised with herbs and spices, though they were certainly a regular medieval dish. But his pike, if caught, will be handled gently, the hook disgorged with the expertise of a surgeon, and the long slimy creature, albeit spotted and barred most beautifully upon the flanks with primrose spots and bars, will be slid into the river to swim away none the worse, but perhaps a little wiser, about the angler's wiles.

Schoolboys love pike fishing. I did a lot of it as a boy. There was something thrilling about the sudden disappearance of the pike bung and those tingling twelve seconds before you lifted the rod butt to drive the hooks home. For a pike does not usually mess about with the bait, not if he is of any size. He seizes your hapless roach impaled on the hooks through flank and fin and bears it away like a shark, holding it crosswise in those dreadful needled jaws before bolting it down into his capacious gullet.

Our old gardener of my boyhood days, Perkins, the successor to old bearded Gunn, was a valiant piker. Every Saturday in winter and autumn he would be down by the lower pool, well wrapped up in his old top coat, a pipe in his mouth, hoping for a bite. He really was a true hunter, for the pike he caught were consumed at home with relish.

There was one big fish, which he hooked and lost on several occasions, whose weight was estimated at double figures. Yet one March day (March was the best time to catch a really big pike) he hooked and landed it and brought it up to the house in triumph. By pike standards it was small, little over eight pounds if I remember right, but victory was complete, the jubilation great.

I recently wrote a piece about big pike in one of our leading sporting journals and I had in return a most interesting letter from the son of Jim Vincent, the famous Broadland keeper to Lord Desborough. He told me how his father, who had caught some very big pike in his time, fish over twenty pounds, once hooked the veritable grand-daddy of them all.

He had with him his boatman, one Ted Piggin, a giant of a man. When Jim Vincent had the great fish beaten and rolling by the boat Piggin reached out with the gaff, but the weight of the fish was daunting. Piggin took another grip on the shaft of the gaff, a fatal move, for the hooks came away as the line pressure eased and away went the leviathan.

Edwin Vincent told me that he was in at the kill of another great fish on Horsey Mere when he was fishing in company with a Mr Peter Hancock. This time there was no mistake, the fish was brought to boat. Edwin had recently purchased a new fish scale from Hardy's and that went down with a bump when the fish was weighed so it may well have been over forty pounds.

It was, according to Edwin, a magnificent specimen, in the pink of condition and was 'as bright and colourful as a fresh-caught mackerel.' Edwin tried to persuade the successful captor to have it preserved for Norwich Museum but it was returned to the water, to his great sorrow.

He tells me there are now few really big pike in the Broads since the great inrush of the sea when it broke through the fens in the sixties. Though its head is shovel-shaped and the mouth most sinister, with its cruel undershot jaw, the pike is a beautiful creature when in prime condition at the end of winter. The primrose spots and scales along the flanks, the snow-white belly and gills, the strangely shaped tail which always reminds me of the propellers of a liner, all contribute to its impressive appearance.

There have always been tales of giant pike. Perhaps the biggest (stories as well as fish!) come from Ireland. I am not sure what the present record is for the British Isles. In my *Fisherman's Bedside Book* (1945) the record is given as 53 pounds from Loch Conn in Ireland. I believe a heavier fish has been caught since and there is always the wonderful story of the pike found dead in Lillieshall Lime Works Pond in 1765 which weighed 170 pounds, but this is suspect.

Vesey Fitzgerald quotes in my *Fisherman's Bedside Book* two pike of over 70 pounds and County Clare boasts one of 78 pounds which was taken on a fly in 1830, but none of these records is substantiated.

By far the most amusing and undoubtedly true story of a big pike was sent to me (by Vesey Fitzgerald again) for my *Fisherman's Bedside Book*. This was of a three-year-old child playing boats in the lake at Upton House, Edgehill, Warwick-shire, the 'boat' being the head of a croquet mallet. A pike seized this and made off with it and, no doubt panicking, drove aground in some shallows. The child's father, Colonel Fitzgerald, waded out and retrieved both croquet mallet and pike, which was in poor condition. Even so it weighed 40 pounds, was four feet one inch in length, with a girth of twenty-five inches. It was mounted and preserved. I wonder where it is now?

December 1 ——————————————

On my netted sallow tree I can only see *one*
hibernating larva! Even this was doubtful,
for I thought it was a crinkle in the bark
where a branch joined the main stem. It was not
until I touched it very gently and felt it move
that I realized it was a larva. Where the other five have gone I
know not. They may still have to wait until the spring.

There is a depressing gloom about these early days of
winter — dark at four p.m. and lights lit.

At last the leaves are down. The garden presents a desolate
scene with the fallen leaves strewing the lawn. Those that fell
in Big Pond have sunk without trace, the water has taken on
the hue of dark mahogany. Only the oaks are still in leaf; the
colour of the dead leaves is a particularly lovely shade of rich,
red brown — a most rare tint.

I noticed the oaks recently in Scotland. I never realized
how well the oak thrives in Perthshire and the Borders. Fine,
well-grown and sturdy trees grow beside the roads — elms
appear to be absent and ash trees not common.

One evening I went with two friends for the evening flight
to a wonderful place we call the Valley of the Geese. This is
mercifully on a private estate and protected from the attention
of the 'marsh cowboys'. It is only shot three or four times in
the season. I sat with my dog beside me among the dead grass
and thistles by a flood bank next to the river.

Polar my labrador had on his camouflage jacket made out
of an old coat of mine. Being the colour of old ivory, he shows
up from a distance unless we are among dead reeds. He was
alert for every sound, looking about him with eager gaze, his
ears pricked. As it grew dusk he reared himself up on his hind

legs like a kangaroo and I noticed he was looking interestedly at something out in the stubble.

For a while I could see nothing, not even through my binoculars, but he kept on whining and looking back at me as if to say 'can't you see it, stupid?' Then I noticed something moving. It was a hare which was loping along and grazing. Occasionally I could hear a single goose calling, but the grand army was elsewhere. They had been there at dawn but now they had departed — no doubt restless with the absurdly mild weather, for the days in late November had been almost springlike in the autumn of 1980.

Sitting there among the withered stalks of sorrel and thistle, I enjoyed the tranquil twilit scene — the dimming field, the lights springing out in the farm on the hill.

A lone curlew called and plover also.

When it was almost dark a party of six geese passed low over the fence some fifty yards distant. They uttered no sound and alighted on a large, flooded part of the field. I have noticed before that wild geese — when in a family party (wild geese keep together as a family all through the winter) — rarely call when coming in to an inland roost. One would have thought that down the centuries they would have learnt to keep silent, but when in skein they always converse and this is so often their undoing, you can hear them a mile away.

Darker grew the field — the stars came blinking, and to the west a line of bare oak trees were outlined against the last wan gleam of day. I found contentment and pleasure in such moments even though I had not had a shot. The smell of the damp grass and weeds, the furtive sound of passing duck — that low 'mutter-mutter' so typical of flight time, and the thin keening of the green plover who were moving down to the flood. These things I relished.

My friend Mac, who was at the far end by the line of trees, had not fired a shot all evening, but as I got up to go I heard him fire and distinctly heard the thump as a goose hit the bank. It was the last shot of his trip and he was pleased about it. A single bird had come past him in the dusk.

As for the family party on the flood they departed as silently as they arrived. When I walked back across the stubble I heard them lift from the water and glimpsed dark wings vanishing into the night.

From September to April this valley is musical with the wild geese — all greylags, who roost on the huge flat fields near the river — sometimes their numbers swell to many thousands and the first arrive before mid-September — the vanguard of the big skeins which arrive from the north in October.

As long as there is a measure of protection against disturbance they will continue to do so — long may they come there. The very occasional shooting party does not disturb them unduly; the number must be culled for too many geese do considerable damage to winter wheat and rape. This has posed problems in Norfolk and the east coast where Brent geese — protected now for some years — raid the farmers' fields in ever-increasing numbers.

Their staple food — the 'zos' or eel grass which grows below the tide line — is less plentiful than formerly, probably due to toxic waste from industrial areas. The Brents have found more succulent pickings inland on the fields of winter wheat; their feeding habits seem to be changing.

A friend who farms on the Holkham Estates in Norfolk tells me that he has been plagued with Brent geese for the last two years and nothing but shooting will scare them away. 'Bangers' and scarecrows work for a time but are then ignored. It is a curious little goose with an almost reptilian head. On the table it is far less palatable than the pinkfoot or greylag.

My two tame cock bullfinches, which I reared from the nest six years ago, gave me a great welcome when I returned from Scotland recently. They were genuinely delighted to see me again and spent all day whistling the tunes I have taught them.

I was sent a most interesting account the other day of two hen bullfinches using the same nest — an account of this appeared in *British Birds*, October 1980. The nest was in a small pine in Lancashire. When found, it contained nine eggs.

Some had a pale blue base whilst others were much lighter.

Two hens were seen to arrive at the nest and after much pushing and shoving both settled down to brood. There appeared to be only one male bird which fed each hen in turn — calling them to him with a soft low pipe. Unfortunately, the nest was robbed by a predator when the eggs were near hatching. I once found a bullfinch's nest with eight eggs and now wonder if two females were involved.

No hedgerow bird suffers from the predators as much as the bullfinch. The nest is usually built near the ground some four feet or so up — usually in sloe bushes or hawthorn. I found one once in a holly. The structure is frail and often almost as transparent as that of the woodpigeon, and the eggs can be seen showing through the lining, which is invariably of slender roots and horsehair — never wool or feathers. Very occasionally they will build a substantial nest with a thick outer 'skin' of twigs cunningly interlaced.

I think that the modern method of cutting hedges by machine helps the bullfinch, for then the twigs and thorns are cropped close, but even so mice will raid the nests. Weasels raid nests too, though mice are the chief predators.

December 5

On a clear afternoon in midwinter the low sun casts long 'evening' shadows acros the quiet fields. There is no warmth in its pale rays, yet the stubbles as yet unploughed, and the ragged hedgerows, show warm tints — sometimes almost ruddy where berries hang on bare twigs, and even the dead bleached grass takes on a warm glow and there is a purple bloom on the hedges.

So it was this afternoon — not a cloud all day, a promise of frost at night, and the blackbirds and thrushes puffed out against the winter cold, turning over the dead leaves in search of insects. On a field of rape some three or four hundred lapwings sat in a compact mass enjoying the sun's rays — they showed up like pale stones on the field. On a large, green, south-facing hill above the Eye Brook reservoir sat a great concourse of Canada geese appearing from a distance like a compact flock of sheep.

They too were enjoying the winter sun, each with a stout breast turned towards the feeble rays. Now and again other small parties of geese lifted from the reservoir and, with stately flogging flight, crossed low over the road and boundary hedge to join the main gaggle on the field.

All wild geese delight to sun themselves, though I do not class Canadas as really 'wild'. I have seen a large gaggle of pink-footed geese in Scotland basking like this on a southern mountain slope — not one of them feeding (most with in-tucked heads or idly preening), and all sitting down, though one or two sentries stood to keep watch.

There are so many Canadas now in the Midland area and Norfolk that they are truly feral, but no wild goose would have crossed that road at a height of ten feet! They are dignified and handsome fowl, greatly prized as a sporting bird in USA and Canada. I can never like them as much as the pinks and greylags; the same applies to the mute swan as opposed to the wild swans. My own colony of house-sparrows also enjoy the late-winter sun. I see them sitting on the old curved tiles of my studio and on top of the weeping cherry, always — like the geese and plovers — facing the sun. There they sit, preening and gossiping.

House-sparrows can be maddening when they interfere with my nesting swallows. They oust the house-martins from their nests but I must confess I have a weakness for them, if only for their sturdy survival tactics and their resolute fight for existence. It is perhaps the most hardy bird alive — adaptable and prolific breeders all over the world.

My attitude to them has changed. I must confess I now feed them each morning with chick pellets! They sit within a few inches of me, puffed and smiling. We have buried our differences, a winter truce has been declared, but they interfere with my studio swallows at their peril.

I remember the old man I once saw in a Paris park with sparrows perching all over him — on head and shoulders, as he walked along. Perhaps in time I will win that same confidence.

Opposite my house across the road is a large field of rape. In the mornings — soon after sun up, the pheasants appear from the forest. I counted twenty-two this morning, creeping along half hidden by the leaves, pecking not at the rape but at the small 'second growth' of corn shoots, for it was a wheat field last summer. By eleven o'clock there was not one to be seen, all had returned to the forest or had wandered off into cover in the hedgerows.

The forest is so vast and thick that they can find secure refuge there and are difficult to shoot by anyone standing in the narrow rides, for they will not take wing. Like the foxes they give all hunters the slip — the foxes by running in circles, the pheasants by dodging away under the thick thorns. By sundown all the 'day' birds are at roost, they face a long night at midwinter — all of twelve hours, far more than humans.

The rooks go to their favourite roosting wood — the wrens and tits to cosy holes in stack, brickwork, or hollow trees, the thrushes and blackbirds to the thick old thorn hedges and ivy. On a moonlit night one can see them up in the tangled twigs, round black balls — a very cold and draughty dormitory indeed.

Recently, when walking back from duck flighting in Scotland, I disturbed numberless redwings and fieldfares which were roosting in tall stubble. It would seem a strange place to roost on the frosty ground, but the thick-cut stems of corn stubble give shelter from the keen wind. The wild geese — hardiest of birds — scorn shelter and will sit out on the sand banks or on the low river fields in the hardiest weather. Their woolly 'undies' render them impervious to cold.

With the sun shining from a cloudless sky one would think there was heat in it, but step into the shadow of the tall thorn hedge and you feel the cold — the grass there on the shadow side is white and furred all day. Even in full sunlight of December you need a warm coat.

This is when the bright yellow stars of the winter jasmine give such pleasure (a strange season to come into flower), and my winter flowering prunus is beginning to bloom. In a week or so it will be as white as may unless a hard frost singes the blossom.

With a little thought it is possible to plan a complete winter garden which will provide bloom all through the dark days, for there are other plants and trees which flower in our English winters. Once Christmas is passed there are early flowering crocus, snowdrop, and aconite. The winter-flowering heathers are not affected by frost.

It may seem a strange thing to say, but I can enjoy an old English hedgerow more in winter than in summer. The ancient tall thorn hedges growing beside roads and along the headlands of the fields show their fine sturdy main stems sometimes festooned with ivy and, higher up, the intricate maze of twigs, where the old nests of summer birds are still intact. The wild hop — or old man's beard — climbs to the very top of the highest branch — sometimes ascending the smaller ash saplings. The silvery filaments are draped gracefully over the hedges, giving a frosty effect.

You can see into the hedgebottoms too in winter, now the grass and weeds are down. In summer all is hidden in a dense canopy of leaves.

It is in these dry hedge bottoms that the rabbits have their snug 'forms', for since myxamatosis they have taken to living above ground. Wild bryony berries, luscious and scarlet, shine like precious stones, and the bright orange red of the hips make a brilliant splash of colour, providing a nice contrast to the deep tapestry-red colour of the hawthorn berries.

Those hedges which are cut by machine lose all character and are as uninteresting as a suburban privet hedge. In time, if the hawthorns are not laid or cut, they will grow into separate trees, useless as a barrier to stock but pleasant on the eye, and in time will grow to their full height of thirty feet or so.

The fieldfares and redwings rely on the berries to see them through the winter. The former are handsome thrushes with their boldly striated breasts and flanks — rich brown back, pale rumps, and dark tails. It always puzzles me why these birds, denizens of the far norhtern pine forests, are so shy of man. They cannot be unduly persecuted in their wild and remote habitats, yet they are as fearful of man as any sporting bird.

Like many other British species they are now far less numerous in the Midlands. I remember as a boy seeing vast flocks feasting in the winter hedgerows. The low 'chuck-a-chuck' call note was one of the most poignant sounds of this dead time of the year, sure message that winter had arrived. It is a sound which makes the sportsman think of his gun, and the primitive hunter stirs within him. The frosty red orb sinking over the bare stubble, the keen 'sliced apple' tang of frost, are enough to set the wildfowler planning his foray after the wild geese, he cannot wait to be up and away. A primitive quarry in all truth, for to early man a wild goose would really have been something to bring home to the thatched hut or cave; there would have been much rejoicing among the women and children.

In those times wild geese would not be easy to secure with primitive weapons. The bow would have been a bit tricky — you would have to show yourself, the aim must be taken at leisure. They might have used nets, perhaps, and cunningly set springes and nooses, or the simplest trap of all — that used in Ireland — of a hole dug in the ground the size of a goose, and a little deeper than his bill or his long neck could reach. At the bottom of the cavity is the bait, grain. The goose overreaches himself and is trapped upside down, his wings held close by the sides of the hole. At least — that is the idea — it sounds Irish. Payne Galway swears it was effective, and he should know.

Even to the student naturalist these primitive urges to hunt are nothing to be ashamed of, they are signs of healthy masculinity which nearly all women and some city-bred males cannot understand or experience.

Recently — on a cold dawn in Scotland — I waited in ambush beside a tree-girt burn. When the greylags flighted I took my three birds and let the others in easy range go unsaluted. I abominate those so-called sportsmen who delight in killing large bags of wild geese and duck at a single flight.

Moderation in all things — there lies the key to true enjoyment.

December 10

I have just been watching a tractor ploughing one of the water meadows beside the Nene. It was a scene which gave some interest to one of those days of unyielding gloom when a sad mist veiled fields and woods and the air was chill.

This particular meadow is an awful gamble from the farmer's point of view as he never knows when it will be transformed into a glittering lake of vast dimensions; even the road on which I was walking is impassable to traffic at least once or twice a year. At such times these flat meadows are the haunt of numberless wildfowl, gulls, waders, and on rare occasions, geese. In severe weather I have even seen whooper swans. Less than half a century ago whitefronted geese were regular winter visitors, but they have not been seen now for many years.

Watching this tractor toiling across the flat expanse I realized what a boon it was for the attendant gull flocks who followed behind in a flickering white cloud, just as one sees the gulls at sea following a fishing boat. Stooping again and again, they pick up the rich harvest of worms, gorging themselves to capacity and then, when more than replete, they adjourned to a nearby green field to digest, sitting in a compact white mass, for an hour or more. This is the usual habit of these inland gulls. At dawn they seek out some field which is being ploughed and remain there all day, repairing to the nearest reservoirs for sleep — it is their regular programme in winter.

I stood beside the bare hedge and watched the tractor lurching upon its way to the far misty limit and back again, right to the road where I was standing, and was amused to see that others beside gulls were taking advantage of this wonderful iron animal which spread a continuous dinner table for hungry mouths.

No less than thirteen pied wagtails were busy at the plough tail, picking up all sorts of insects and grubs which were being thrown up by the shares. Like the insect-eating birds of Africa, the plovers and members of the crane family who follow the grazing rhinos, buffalo and elephants, these wagtails were no different, they did not associate a man with the lurching tractor, nor did the gulls.

To insect-eating birds the plough is really a godsend in winter for in few other ways could they get enough to eat, especially in hard weather. Even little birds like wrens might benefit, though I have never seen these little people following a plough — they keep to the hedgerows.

In a few years I understand these water meadows will be no more for beneath the soil and not far down is a rich strata of gravel. Soon all those flat bird-haunted pastures will be transformed, first into gaping pits busy with shovels and mechanical diggers, then to vast expanses of rippling water no doubt good for anglers, but not for the wildfowl, for gravel excavations are mostly too deep for ducks and herons and only serve as roosting places. Yet for some reason hard to fathom I never see large rafts of roosting duck on flooded gravel pits; they seem to prefer the reservoirs, possibly because most have large margins of shallow water and boggy places such as to be found at the Eye Brook reservoir and the magnificent Rutland Water.

One puzzling thing which always intrigues me, is that these flooded gravel pits in the valley of the Nene are never utilized as a water supply. They are of considerable depth and must contain millions of gallons of pure water over a clean gravelly bottom. There is a heronry not far distant and the ground all around it is now being excavated — soon it will be on an island. The herons do not approve of all the noisy activity and last spring there were fewer nests. When the work is done and the pits are full of water they will no doubt return in their usual numbers.

198

At about this time of year, the Eye Brook, is a fascinating place for the bird-watcher. Every weekend one sees people with binoculars lining the adjacent road. The most spectacular thing to my mind are the immense numbers of gulls which start coming back to roost about an hour before sundown. All day they have been harvesting the 'plough share', and as the sun begins to dip towards the western hills you can see the birds drifting in in ones and twos from all parts of the compass.

Some may be coming from many miles distant and as the sun sinks, the surface of the water appears to be carpeted with white snow. To count this vast concourse would be impossible as, even when dusk cloaks the fields, the gulls still keep arriving, possibly those from a long distance. They must be counted in millions not thousands, as I have seen the whole top arm literally blanketed with a solid white sheet of gulls. No doubt the droppings feed the fish but such great numbers of sleeping birds must foul the water.

A quarter of the reservoir at its northern end is shallow. Most summers it dries right out and cattle graze there. It is a wonderful haunt of wigeon packs which come in their hundreds each winter. As the gulls come in drifting like ghosts, half seen in the fast fading light, the wigeon and mallard flight out, so one can witness a two way traffic.

I have no doubt if wild ducks (and wigeon also) were not persecuted they would copy the gulls in their plough-following tactics. But the wigeon are mostly grazers and fly off up the valley of the Welland which is a famous grazing ground for cattle and where some of the sweetest grass in the whole of the country grows. Welland beef is famous throughout the land, for it possesses properties which I understand are unique for fattening beasts and giving flavour to the meat. The sporting farmers of this rich valley, like the farmers of that haunted land of Sedgemoor, can enjoy magnificent flighting. Many a fine fat mallard and wigeon falls to their guns as they ambush the birds from behind the willows and ditches in the winter twilights. It is inland fowling of the highest order, though without the romance of the coast. In late September, teams of ducks follow the winding course of lazy Welland Water, outlined against the pale evening skies; most are bound for the barley stubbles on the higher fields on either side of the valley.

Some years ago my wife and I, plus daughter, made a leisurely summer trip by boat all down the Nene to where it joins the fens. We spent many weeks on the journey, anchoring here and there in quiet willow-girt reaches. We were fortunate in having a lovely summer. We never went far each day, not more than a mile or so, and in the evening I used to fish off the stern of our boat and catch many a dish of delicious dace which we fried like whitebait, little finger-long fish, dry and rustly, hot from the grill.

The locks of the Nene are frequent and some we found hard to open and shut, yet what a peaceful time that was, gliding along through buttercup meadows. One photo I took shows us anchored under some willows near a field ablaze with a sea of golden buttercups.

We began our journey in May and it did not finish until the autumn. What a lazy leisurely existence that was, far from roads and traffic! I wrote a book about this journey called *A Summer on the Nene* which is, alas!, out of print. From outside Northampton to the outskirts of Peterborough the river passes through delightful country, and we had very few days when the rain kept us anchored and frustrated. A small boat is no place in which to be cooped when the weather is bad, but time passed quickly as I had the book to write. I did so as we journeyed on.

Now for quite another subject, *tobacco pipes*. I have always enjoyed my pipe (not cigarettes, which are quite abhorrent to me — for the smell of burning paper and finely shredded tobacco is quite unpleasant, apart from damaging your health). I have never been without my pipe, save for a lapse of a year when I decided smoking was a waste of money. I held out against temptation for quite twelve months, then, when walking down the main street of Fort William, a man passed me smoking my favourite brand. I turned in at the next tobac-conist's shop and bought a pipe and a packet of my chosen brand, and I have smoked ever since. But I limit myself to four pipes a day and never smoke between meals.

One can pay a great deal for a pipe. My favourite is a cheap thick-bowled cherrywood. Cherrywood gives a subtle flavour to the weed but such are hard to come by these days. Most cherrywoods one sees in the shops have bowls that are far too thin, and the result is that one gets a hot dry smoke.

When my present pipe disintegrates (it shows signs of doing so) I must try and cut one for myself if I can find somebody to turn the bowl for me. Many of the thick old cherrywoods were made in France. Why one cannot get one now I do not know, unless it is something to do with the Common Market.

Nearly all the old wildfowlers I knew never favoured cigarettes, always a pipe. Many a quiet smoke have I enjoyed in their company when waiting for the fowl to fly at that magic time of the first star.

December 15

I find, as I grow older, that time takes on a new significance and is something to be cherished. One becomes more aware of the rhythm of the days — night comes too soon for me and I find myself wondering how I have employed myself during the day. Sometimes the precious hours have been wasted, frittered away with no creative work and not even the enjoyment of a good book or country walk.

A lot of time can be wasted in sleep. What a precious thing it is — this 'time' which slips away so inexorably second by second. Clock and watchmakers get so used to the sound of time ticking away that they give the subject no thought at all. I have discussed this subject with them.

When on a Saturday night I wind up the old grandfather clock, I remember my father used to do so for the last forty years of his life. As a small boy in bed on a Saturday night I could hear the grinding noise as the heavy weights were pulled upwards. Now my own child hears that sound. The ancient clock-face — eighteenth century — is a measuring stick which measures life.

I sometimes wish there were no such things as clocks to give audible reminder of the passing seconds and no such things as calendars or diaries. Then I remember the rising and setting of the sun is a measuring stick; each nightfall, a tick of a clock.

Youth, that glorious dawning, does not notice time. We never gave it a thought, and rightly so. To the child, time is non-existent. It is only when we realize our own life must end that it takes on a new significance. That knowledge came as a terrible shock to me. I was seven or eight at the time, and for days a cloud hung over me which has never gone away completely. I have described this realization in my book *A Child Alone*.

December 16 _____

The red-barked willows by Big Pond are becoming a brighter hue every day. By March they will be brilliant. As soon as they start to shoot in April I cut all the scarlet wands back, leaving a few inches, and they then bush out even thicker. If left uncut their stems lose their colour and become yellow.

Grouped near water these willows make a brave splash of colour all through the winter months. Like all the willow family they are the easiest of all to root. Cut off a bunch of them above a bud, thrust them well home in the ground and they will root, especially in damp ground. Sallows also are easy to root if the wands are cut in February. Anyone wishing for a quick-growing tree or bush can do no better than plant sallow, and in the spring the silver buds are most attractive, especially those of the goat willow with their golden-powdered buds so beloved by the early bees. A good-sized sallow wand of some three feet or more will grow into a sizable tree in a couple of years. When one is past middle age this is an advantage.

December 22

There had been snow in the night. It still lay in the shadowed parts of the woodland ride, printed here and there with the three-toed spoor of pheasants. The afternoon sun shone upon the naked spires of the larch trees, giving the stems and twigs a golden glow, but where I walked I was in cold shadow from the dark-tasselled firs.

Empty cartridge cases lay in the frosty grass, relics of a recent shoot. The sticks with their numbered labels still fixed in the split tops, showing where the guns had stood, each peg surrounded by a ring of empty cases.

I took a narrow pathway down on my right, glimpsing through the trees the winding river, which was a vivid blue reflecting the clear sunlit sky above. I intended to make my way along the water meadows to the stone bridge close to the empty Hall, standing among its cedars on the opposite hill.

Crawling under the barbed wire I found myself in the spacious green water meadows, peewit haunted, which 'go under' in times of flood. The Nene, even though controlled by locks, still floods the whole valley after heavy winter rains.

I did not progress very far before I was brought up short by quaking boggy ditches filled with dead rush from which snipe arrowed away, exploding from the marshy tussocks with the alarm note 'scaape scaape'. I tried to cross in several places and at last managed to jump one ditch with the help of a sunken log.

Beyond, the grass seemed firm and green but I had not gone more than a dozen yards before the way was barred by yet another slough of despond, so I had to go back into the thick wood, pushing my way among the rusty stalks of willow herb, burr, brambles, and the white forests of dead nettle stalks.

In summer I could not have found a path through, and as

it was I had to fight my way through the briers which were almost as impenetrable as barbed wire. The whipping tendrils of the brier with their armoured spines catch the clothes and hold one fast. But I pushed on, seeing the radiant sun burning before me through the stems of the larches.

Then quite suddenly I came upon the 'Folly' — a towering structure of stone with a high arch above. It had been erected, I suppose, at the end of the eighteenth century, when 'follies' were all the fashion with the big landowners. I suppose the building of them relieved the boredom of those days — possibly the old lord himself designed this 'folly'.

I could visualize him in his warm library with the roaring fire, his dogs about him, pencil and ruler to hand. What a 'phoney' erection it was, this sham ruin! No doubt — on his travels in Italy and Germany he had seen such ruins when he made the 'grand tour'.

I stood among the brambles looking up at the stone arch above me. Ivy had climbed up it — it stood dark against the tender evening light for now the sun was almost down. Pheasants were cocking up to roost in the larches all about me.

Not far distant, beyond the wood, was the church with its tall spire. Legend has it that this church once stood near the Hall and on Sundays the village, going to worship, had to pass within sight of the Hall windows. So the old lord decided the church should be moved, and so it was, stone by stone, to its new site a mile distant, well out of sight of aristocratic gaze.

Quickly the light in the western sky faded. I fought my way out of the wood at last to the open hill above the river, thankful to leave the tangled wilderness to its rightful tenants, the roosting pheasants, the foxes and the owls who were already beginning to salute the coming night, owl answering owl all along that wooden hill.

Below was the winding river, bright still but no longer blue, a coiling ribbon of paleness set in the quiet fields. A team of ducks went flying against the western sky, a compact bunch, with the location of their night's dinner table firmly in their brains, for they flew with urgency and on a steady compass course.

A day or so to the shortest day! It seemed almost unbelievable, how swiftly my year had gone.

It had been a happy one.